# Kiddiwalks

## NEAR
## BRISTOL & BATH

◆◆◆◆◆◆◆◆◆◆◆◆◆◆◆◆◆◆◆◆◆◆◆◆◆

## Nigel Vile

COUNTRYSIDE BOOKS
NEWBURY BERKSHIRE

COUNTRYSIDE  BOOKS
3 Catherine Road
Newbury, Berkshire

To view our complete range of books,
please visit us at
www.countrysidebooks.co.uk

ISBN 978 1 85306 846 1

Designed by Peter Davies, Nautilus Design
Maps by the author
Cover picture supplied by Faith Tillotson
Bird illustrations on page 96 supplied
by Trevor Yorke


Designed by Peter Davies, Nautilus Design
Produced through MRM Associates Ltd., Reading
Typeset by CJWT Solutions, St Helens
Printed by Information Press, Oxford

# Contents

# Contents

**PUBLISHER'S NOTE**

We hope that you obtain considerable enjoyment from this book; great care has been taken in its preparation. Although at the time of publication all routes followed public rights of way or permitted paths, diversion orders can be made and permissions withdrawn.

We cannot, of course, be held responsible for such diversion orders and any inaccuracies in the text which result from these or any other changes to the routes nor any damage which might result from walkers trespassing on private property. We are anxious though that all details covering the walks are kept up to date and would therefore welcome information from readers which would be relevant to future editions.

# Introduction

Being a writer of walking guidebooks, I am often asked for advice or recommendations for routes. This is particularly the case with friends with young families, who as childless couples enjoyed a few hours in the great outdoors, a freedom that parenthood has curtailed. 'It must be a short walk, not too many hills and with something to interest the children.' There is usually a footnote, too, that the walk must have a family-friendly pub or teashop, as much for mum or dad as the children!

The emphasis in this book of 'Kiddiwalks' matches the above specification almost perfectly. Do not expect Herculean treks of Wainwright proportions or you will be sadly disappointed. The objective is to provide relatively short and undemanding walks with a variety of attractions to stimulate the interest of youngsters. It may be the ever-popular stream or river, it could be a long barrow or hillfort, possibly a beach or safe rock scramble. With distances that range from just 1 mile to no more than 3 miles, there are routes here that will suit everyone from toddlers to top juniors, as well as their parents and grandparents.

The area around Bath and Bristol is tremendously rich and varied. To the west lie the Severn Estuary and the Bristol Channel, explored on walks at Sand Point, Clevedon, Severn Beach and Oldbury, whilst the walks at Conham, Willsbridge and Saltford go deep into the heart of the Avon Valley. The Mendip area is featured on the routes at Beacon Batch, Crook Peak and Ebbor, whilst the walks at Westhay, Lower Woods and Brown's Folly explore a number of fine nature reserves. Bathonians and Bristolians are truly blessed in having such a diverse range of natural habitats.

Each walk in the book is presented in as user-friendly a manner as possible. There is firstly an outline of the route, followed by a 'Fact File' recording all of the key information such as the distance and timing for the walk, how to get to the start point and refreshment facilities. The fact file also indicates whether or not the walk is suitable for pushchairs and buggies, as well as the ideal age of child suited to the route in question. There is then a section headed 'Fun Things to See and Do'

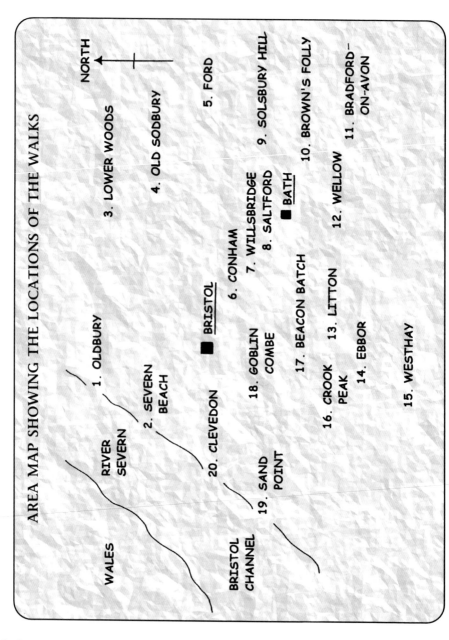

AREA MAP SHOWING THE LOCATIONS OF THE WALKS

NORTH

WALES

RIVER SEVERN

BRISTOL CHANNEL

1. OLDBURY
2. SEVERN BEACH
3. LOWER WOODS
4. OLD SODBURY
5. FORD
6. CONHAM
7. WILLSBRIDGE
8. SALTFORD
9. SOLSBURY HILL
10. BROWN'S FOLLY
11. BRADFORD–ON-AVON
12. WELLOW
13. LITTON
14. EBBOR
15. WESTHAY
16. CROOK PEAK
17. BEACON BATCH
18. GOBLIN COMBE
19. SAND POINT
20. CLEVEDON

BRISTOL

BATH

# Introduction

which details the interest for the children, be it hunting for fossils, clambering on rocks, bird spotting or listening out for animals. The sketch maps that accompany the walk directions are meant to guide you around the route but I do recommend that you also carry the relevant OS map, details of which are also given. These maps are particularly useful for identifying the main features of views. Following on from the walk directions, there are some background notes on the places and sights passed to enhance the enjoyment of the walk.

My own children are now in their teens and early twenties, and have a penchant for rather more demanding routes. Crib Goch and Tryfan in Snowdonia, for example, excite and appeal far more to young adults than a two-mile stroll along a riverbank! These walks, however, were some of their favourites in their formative years, and I sure that it was these short circuits with their 'kiddy-friendly' attractions that instilled in them a love of the great outdoors. It is so important that children are not force-fed adult walks at a young age, or a negative attitude towards walking will be inevitable. With these thoughts in mind, I commend these routes to you and your children.

## Acknowledgement

I would like to thank my own daughter – Katie Vile – for the pen and ink sketches that illustrate a number of these walks. The skills and ideas developed in her 'A' Level Art course have now borne some fruit!

Nigel Vile

# 1

# Oldbury and the Severn

## Sails, Birds and Driftwood

Rriver estuaries are something special because there is always so much to see and this part of the Severn Estuary at Oldbury is no exception. This walk along the river's flood defences is best done at low tide, when the worms and other inhabitants of the salt marsh come to the surface to be devoured by any number of sea birds. Oldbury Pill, an inlet alongside the river, is home to the local sailing club, whose craft add a touch of colour to this watery landscape. A climb to St Arilda's church affords wonderful views across the water towards the Black Mountains and the Brecon Beacons, as well as downstream towards the Severn Bridges, and with a power station thrown in for good measure, this is certainly an outing to savour.

# Oldbury and the Severn

**Getting there** *Follow the A38 north from Bristol, before taking the B4061 road into Thornbury. On the northern outskirts of this small town, follow the minor road on the left signposted to Oldbury. In the village, turn left at the crossroads, and the Anchor Inn is on the left-hand side of the road ahead.*

**Length of walk** 2¹/₂ miles
**Time** Up to 2 hours
**Terrain** A relatively flat walk that is best suited to children aged six or over. Although buggies could negotiate the flat tops of the flood defences, be prepared for the need to carry them on the short stretches of field path.

**Start/Parking** The parking area opposite the Anchor Inn at Oldbury-on-Severn (GR 608923).

**Maps** OS Landranger 172 or OS Explorer 167.

**Refreshments** The Anchor Inn at Oldbury-on-Severn is popular with families. Children are welcome in the eating areas. An alternative would be to take a picnic to enjoy alongside the Severn.

## Fun Things to See and Do ◆

**This is the ideal opportunity** to do some bird spotting as large numbers of wading birds, such as dunlin, curlew and redshank, swoop down here looking for their next meal. At low water, the wildfowl spread themselves out over the exposed mudflats, moving to the upper shore to roost. The ebb and flow of the tides also brings driftwood up to the riverbank, often unusual shaped pieces of timber weathered and worn by the water's power, providing the perfect opportunity for young artists to let their imaginations run wild.

## The Walk

NORTH

OLDBURY
PILL

TO THORNBURY
AND THE A38

RIVER
SEVERN

OLDBURY-
ON-SEVERN

1.
START

2.

COWHILL

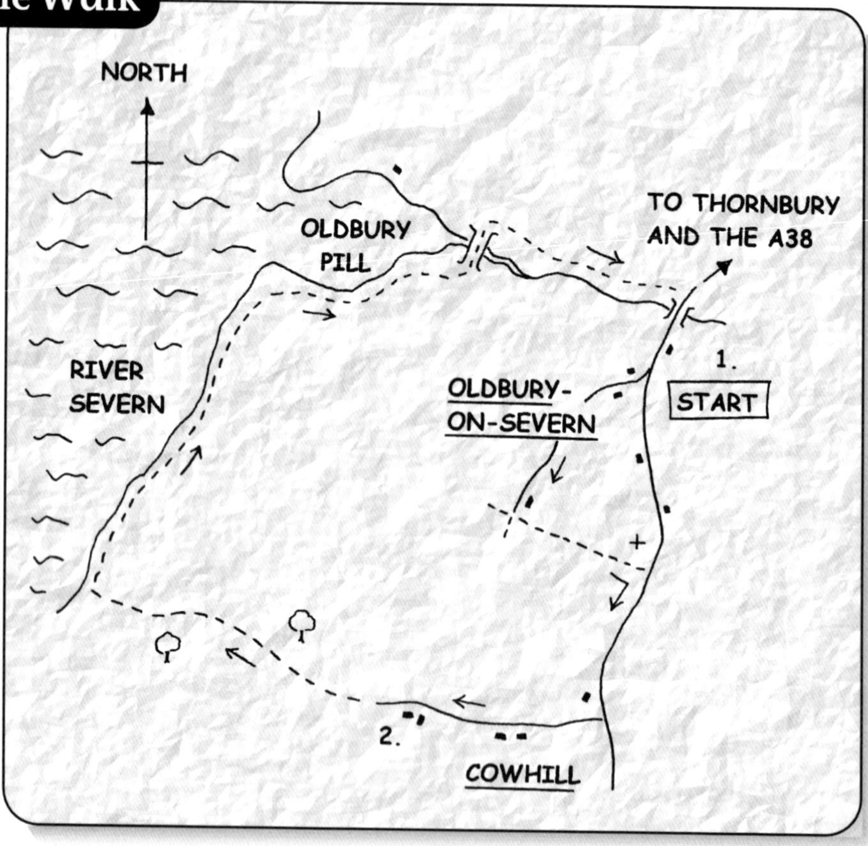

❶ Walk past the Anchor Inn, and take the first turning on the right – Westmarsh Lane. Follow this quiet back road for 1/4 mile and, just before an isolated detached house on the left, turn left to reach a stile. Follow the right edge of the field beyond this stile uphill towards St Arilda's church. Cross the stiles in the top corner of the field, before heading across the next field to a gate just to the right of the church. Join the verge beyond this gate, and follow the lane to the right downhill for 300 yards into Cowhill, detouring initially to explore the church. In Cowhill, turn right and follow a cul-de-sac lane for 600 yards down past

# Oldbury and the Severn

Manor Farm and Lower Farm.

❷ Beyond Lower Farm, continue along a track for ¼ mile to reach a gate and open field. Cross to the right corner of this field, before climbing the flood defence embankment to reach the banks of the Severn. Turn right, and follow the flood defence northwards for ½ mile in the direction of Oldbury Power Station. Keep on the flood defence as it bears right to follow Oldbury Pill and the yacht moorings. Continue along to a sluice, cross Oldbury Pill and immediately drop down to the grassy area on the right alongside the river. Follow Oldbury Pill upstream for 200 yards, join the access road leading away from the sailing club and continue ahead to a gate and the lane by the Anchor Inn.

## Background Notes ◆

**Oldbury-on-Severn** actually lies some distance from the river. Until the 17th century, however, it was only separated from the treacherous tidal waters of the Severn by undrained and often flooded marshland. The 17th century saw the beginnings of drainage along the riverbank, and a series of rhines turned the marsh into pasture and apple orchard. The village inns, the Ship and the Anchor, speak of links with the river when, in years gone by, Welsh coal was brought across the estuary to Oldbury.

**Oldbury Nuclear Power Station** was constructed between 1961 and 1965. Although a slight diversion from the route, there is a visitor centre, which provides interpretative displays relating to both Oldbury Power Station and the nuclear power industry. The towers holding the actual reactors are over 60 feet in height, and loom large over the river.

**The River Severn** rises on the eastern slopes of Plynlimmon, deep in mid-Wales, where its 210-mile journey through Shrewsbury, Worcester and Gloucester to the Bristol Channel commences. At Oldbury, the river is tidal, and for centuries was the site of salmon fishing. Racks of conical-shaped baskets – or 'putchers' – were placed in the river with their open ends facing upstream. The aim was to capture the salmon on the ebb tide as they migrated through the estuary. This technique of fishing has prehistoric origins and is unique to the Severn. Putchers are usually on display in the Anchor Inn, whose colourful sign illustrates the local salmon fishermen at work.

# 2

# Severn Beach and the Severn Estuary

## Mudflats and Bridges

A few miles north-west of Bristol is the city's very own beach. The sea defences alongside this part of the Severn Estuary offer a bracing stroll and there is the opportunity to view the magnificent Second Severn Crossing and call in at its fascinating visitor centre. The walk can be rounded off with a stop at a traditional seaside café for that welcome ice-cream.

# Severn Beach and the Severn Estuary

**Getting there** *Leave the M48 at junction 1 – near the Old Severn Bridge – and follow the A403 towards Avonmouth. In 3 miles, turn onto the B4064 for Redwick and Severn Beach. In just 1 mile, in Severn Beach itself, follow a short one-way system to the point where Beach Road joins Station Road. Turn right at this junction, heading towards the promenade, and park somewhere in the vicinity of Shirley's Café.*

**Length of walk** 2 miles
**Time** Allow 1½ hours
**Terrain** A user-friendly route, ideally suited for buggies and pushchairs, as well as youngsters of all ages, as the walk follows a concrete sea defence from Severn Beach to New Passage.
**Start/Parking** Beach Road in Severn Beach (GR 530848).
**Maps** OS Landranger 172 or OS Explorer 154.
**Refreshments** Shirley's Café in Station Road at Severn Beach is a traditional – but most welcome – seaside café.

## Fun Things to See and Do ◆

**This is the chance to collect** some pebbles on the beach and to watch out for all manner of birds that visit this shoreline. Cormorant, shelduck and mallard can be spotted all year around, and at certain times of the year a good scattering of species use the river as a migration route, including terns and kittiwakes. Children (and adults) will also enjoy the nearby visitor centre that tells the story of the building of the second bridge that opened in 1996 to provide a much needed additional road crossing from England to Wales.

# Kiddiwalks near Bristol & Bath

## The Walk

for 600 yards to reach the truncated remains of New Passage Pier, just past the rather impressive Severn Lodge Farm.

❷ Retrace your steps back to Severn Beach. For a slight variation, just south of New Passage Pier, fork right onto a lower level concrete walkway that runs just below the sea wall, rejoining the main promenade just by the Second Severn Crossing. Follow the promenade for 40 yards and, just past a radar compound,

❶ Continue walking along Station Road and up onto the promenade at Severn Beach. Turn right, and follow the promenade for ³/₄ mile to reach the Second Severn Crossing. To visit the Severn Bridges Visitor Centre, follow the signposted path on the right at this point. For the main walk, continue following the promenade

rejoin the lower level walkway and follow this alternative route back to the fringes of Severn Beach. Ahead, a stepped flood defence runs below the promenade. Follow this stepped flood defence alongside the beach and, where it ends, turn left along the promenade to return to Station Road.

# Severn Beach and the Severn Estuary

◆◆◆◆◆◆◆◆◆◆◆◆◆◆◆◆◆◆◆◆◆◆◆◆◆◆◆◆

## Background Notes ◆

**Severn Beach:** 'Beach' is actually something of a misnomer, with the foreshore being little more than mud and pebbles bordering the Severn Estuary ... but the word certainly would have helped in the marketing of the resort! With the development of the railway network, Severn Beach was touted as Bristol's equivalent of Blackpool or Southend. The railway arrived here in 1922, and thousands of visitors flocked to the little resort for evening excursions and Bank Holiday day trips. A swimming pool was built, and part of the sea wall was turned into a promenade. There was even a funfair, but it never came anywhere near to rivalling Blackpool's Golden Mile.

With the advent of the motorcar, the working classes could set their sights further afield when it came to leisure trips and excursions. Severn Beach fell into decline – and decay – and the various attractions faced inevitable bankruptcy. The railway from Bristol still survives, but it is a pale shadow of its glorious past. The vast platforms that once welcomed hundreds of day-trippers are now little more than derelict slabs of concrete.

From Severn Beach, a coastal path runs northwards past the Second Severn Crossing and the Severn Bridges Visitor Centre, to **New Passage**. This is the site of a truncated pier, the terminus of the former South Wales Union Railway, where passengers would disembark for ferries to Portskewett in Wales. Amongst the famous travellers to pass this way were John and Charles Wesley on their journeys to Wales and Ireland. Rather more lavish plans to run regular transatlantic steamers to and from the United States, with a rail link to London, never saw the light of day.

**The Second Severn Crossing** is quite simply a magnificent monument to today's engineers. The statistics alone will impress any child – the overall length of the crossing is 5,128 metres with 320,000 cubic metres of concrete used in its construction. Over 1,000 workers were employed between 1992 and 1996 in building the bridge, whose main span lies some 40 metres above the water level. The **Severn Bridges Visitor Centre** contains displays relating to both the Second Severn Crossing and the nearby Severn Bridge. The exhibition covers not only the history of crossing the Severn Estuary, but also the environmental impact that construction work had on the river. A short video brings the construction story to life.

# 3

# Lower Woods

## *If You Go Down To The Woods Today ...*

A quiet lane runs across country from Wickwar towards Hawkesbury and beyond a cattle grid the unfenced byway crosses the open expanses of Inglestone Common. With the occasional cottage and farm set against a backdrop of the Cotswold escarpment, it is a truly delightful setting. Adding to the scene is Lower Woods, the most extensive semi-natural woodland in the Bath and Bristol region, whose boundaries have remained unchanged for several centuries. The range of woodland types is home to a rich array of flora, as well as a variety of bird and mammal populations.

**Getting there** *A minor road runs across country from the B4060 at Wickwar to Hawkesbury Upton. Midway between these two settlements, the lane crosses Inglestone Common. Opposite Inglestone Farm, follow a gravelled track into Lower Woods where, in 600 yards, there is a parking area opposite Long Woods Lodge by an information board.*

**Length of walk** 2 miles
**Time** Allow about 1½ hours for the walk.
**Terrain** Many of the woodland paths on this walk are bumpy

## Fun Things to See and Do ◆

**Woodlands are magical places**, with their secretive glades, and Lower Woods is no exception. Deer are frequent visitors to the rides and tracks although they are extremely timid creatures so it may take a lot of patient waiting before actually spotting one! Spring is an excellent time to come down to the woods, with so many wild flowers carpeting the ground. Wood anemones and celandines, primroses and bluebells are but the most common ones to look out for. And something rather special lives at the northern edges of Lower Woods – the nightingale. This elusive bird can be heard from the dense scrub along the woodland edge for just a few weeks around late April. However, you will have to be in the woodland either at dawn or dusk to hear the magnificent chorus that this fine creature produces. If you are very lucky, you could hear up to 20 singing birds in full song.

The Little Avon River flows through the heart of the woodland, too. Lift the stones in its shallow waters and all manner of tiny creatures might well appear. With so much to look out for, it is a good opportunity to play a variation of the alphabet game. Children love a challenge, so help them to list any flowers or creatures from A-Z as and when they are spotted.

## The Walk

NORTH

WICKWAR
AND THE
B4060

INGLESTONE
FARM

PLUMBER'S
TRENCH

HAWKESBURY
UPTON AND
THE A46

1.

START

WETMOOR
WOOD

HORTON
GREAT
TRENCH

BURNT
WOOD

2.

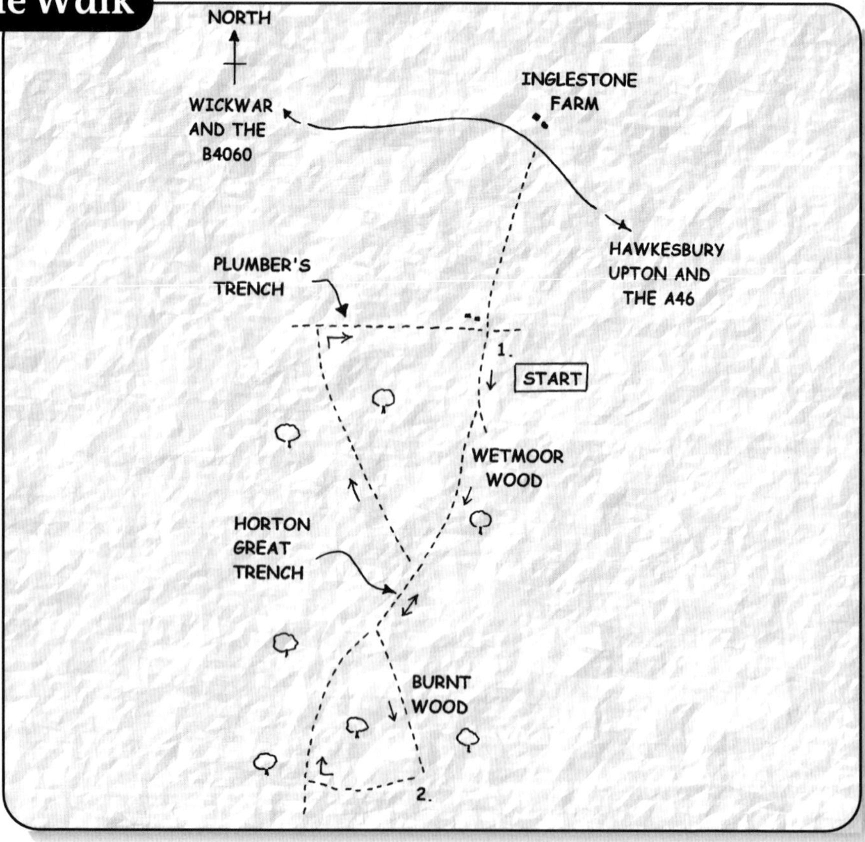

and occasionally rutted, so it is best suited to children who enjoy walking, although they may well welcome an occasional piggyback.

**Start/Parking** The entrance to Lower Woods by Lower Woods Lodge (GR 747881).

**Maps** OS Landranger 172 or OS Explorer 167.

**Refreshments** A picnic would be a great incentive on this walk since there are no refreshment facilities. A pleasant spot would be the common land that surrounds Lower Woods.

# Lower Woods

❶ To the left of the information board is a gate at the entrance to Lower Woods Reserve. Ignore this gate, taking instead the gravelled track running into the woodland just beyond this gateway. In 250 yards, where the track bears left, bear right off of the track to join a grassy ride. Follow this ride downhill for 175 yards to a metal footbridge over the Little Avon River. Cross the river and, beyond the gate ahead, follow a wide grassy ride known as 'Horton Great Trench' for 600 yards to a point where another ride crosses this broad woodland path. Turn left, and follow a track through Burnt Wood – dropping down into and up out of a small valley – before reaching a gate on the left in 500 yards, right on the edge of the wood.

❷ Just before this gate, turn right and follow a track for 375 yards to its junction with Horton Great Trench. Turn right along this ride, and continue for 500 yards to the crosstrack encountered earlier. Continue ahead at this point, retracing your steps along 300 yards of this ride, to an old gateway and track going off on the left, ignoring an earlier pair of paths on the same side of the ride. Follow the path beyond the gateway for 375 yards down to a footbridge over the Little Avon River. Cross the river and follow the ride opposite uphill for 350 yards to Plumber's Trench, a wide crosstrack. Turn right and follow this track for 600 yards to a gateway and the parking area by Lower Woods Lodge.

## Background Notes ◆

Lower Woods are located on the damp, clay soils of the Vale of Berkeley. Crossed by several small streams, including the Little Avon River, the ground is often sticky and waterlogged in the autumn and winter. The site is made up of several woodland blocks, separated by wide tracks or rides that are known locally as 'trenches'. The rides prove attractive to a number of butterfly species that include the white admiral, the silver-washed fritillary and the grizzled skipper. A rich array of flora and fauna are found in the woodland, including deer and hares, tawny owls and kestrels, bluebells and primroses and of course the aforementioned elusive nightingale.

# 4

# *Old Sodbury and the Cotswold Escarpment*

## *Humps and Bumps*

C hildren have boundless energy, and there are enough contour lines and mounds, ditches and ramparts on this walk to burn off just a little of this unspent force! The walk starts from Old Sodbury church, in the lee of the Cotswold escarpment, and straightway there is a fine view across the Severn Vale. A secluded fieldpath is followed through to neighbouring Little Sodbury, before a stiff climb onto the Cotswold hilltops. The strategically located Sodbury Fort, with its vast ramparts and ditches, will prove the perfect place to re-enact a few conflicts from centuries past, before a gentle downhill stroll back into Old Sodbury.

# Old Sodbury and the Cotswold Escarpment

**Getting there** *The A432 heads out through Bristol's north-eastern suburbs, before passing through Yate and Chipping Sodbury en route to the A46 just beyond the village of Old Sodbury. On entering Old Sodbury, turn left by the Dog Inn into Cotswold Lane. At the top of Cotswold Lane, park on the left by the village church. The Dog Inn, incidentally, offers arguably the widest selection of pub food in the area. That must surely be a carrot to dangle in front of tired youngsters – and their parents – during the walk!*

## e Walk

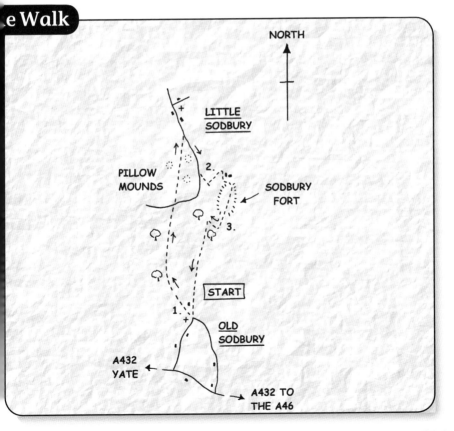

NORTH

LITTLE SODBURY

PILLOW MOUNDS

2.

SODBURY FORT

3.

START

1.

OLD SODBURY

A432 YATE

A432 TO THE A46

# Kiddiwalks near Bristol & Bath

*4*

**Length of walk** 2 miles
**Time** Allow about 1¹/₂ hours.
**Terrain** This route follows mostly fieldpaths and tracks, so pushchairs and buggies, and indeed young toddlers, might struggle on this walk. There is a steep climb above Little Sodbury to reach Sodbury hillfort.

**Start/Parking** Old Sodbury church (GR 756818).
**Maps** OS Landranger 172 or OS Explorer 167.
**Refreshments** The Dog Inn on the A432 in Old Sodbury can boast one of the largest menus in the area! It is also a family-friendly pub.

❶ Walk through the churchyard to a gate in the end boundary wall. Bear half right and head downhill to a pond to the left of a small pylon at the foot of the slope. Turn right, walking above the pond, to a stile in the end field boundary. Follow the right edges of the next three fields to a gateway in the corner of the third field. In the following field, cross to a stile in the far right corner. Cross a lane to a stile opposite and a field containing pillow mounds, and make for a stile in the far right corner and a lane. Detour left to explore Little Sodbury – for the main walk, turn right and follow a lane uphill for 300 yards.

❷ At the top of the hill, turn left along a driveway and, in 20 yards, turn right along a footpath. Just 25 yards along this path, turn left and follow what is the Cotswold Way to the hilltop and a converted farm building. Turn right, walk alongside this

conversion and continue for 20 yards to a gate on the left. Turn left into a field containing Sodbury Fort. Walk ahead for 20 yards, turn right through the ramparts and cross the enclosure to the ramparts opposite. Pass through a gap in the ramparts and continue across the field to a gate to the left of some woodland.

❸ Beyond this gate, turn right and follow an enclosed sunken path downhill. At the foot of the slope,

# Old Sodbury and the Cotswold Escarpment

where this path bears right, pass through a gate on the left and follow the Cotswold Way across the top left edge of a field, with views across the Severn Vale. Pass through a handgate in the far left corner of this field before heading across the next field to a handgate in the corner on the edge of Old Sodbury. Continue along an enclosed path back to Cotswold Lane by Old Sodbury School, and turn right back to the church.

## Fun Things to See and Do ◆

**Old graveyards might be places** associated with ghosts and spirits, but they also tell us lots about history. In the churchyard at Old Sodbury, for example, you can spot a good number of bale-tombs. These tombs were the lavish burial places of rich merchants in the past. Many of the more humble gravestones date back to the early 19th century ... and it will certainly prove a challenge to find any that pre-date 1800. On the hillside outside St John the Baptist's church, there is a special information board called a topograph. This was created to celebrate the new millennium and it helps put the location into some sort of geographical context. Children will have fun spotting such notable landmarks as the New and Old Severn Bridges or Filton Runway. On a clear day, you might be able to pick out the Sugar Loaf in the Black Mountains in Wales, or even the distant peaks of the Brecon Beacons.

On the approach to Little Sodbury is a field covered in a strange collection of shallow bumps and humps. These are shown on the OS maps as 'pillow mounds', artificial mounds created by ancient peoples in the hope of encouraging rabbits to develop vast warrens. This would then provide a steady supply of meat for their dining tables. On the hilltops above Little Sodbury lies a rather more impressive collection of 'bumps' – the ramparts of **Sodbury Fort**, an ideal location to let the children run about, imagining they are the invaders, dodging arrows and stones raining down from above!

# Kiddiwalks near Bristol & Bath

*4*

## ◆ Background Notes ◆

**Old Sodbury church** enjoys a fine location overlooking the Severn Vale. A conveniently placed seat at the western end of the churchyard looks out across neighbouring Chipping Sodbury and the suburbs of Bristol towards the River Severn and the distant Welsh Hills, whilst away to the north stretches the west-facing Cotswold escarpment. St John the Baptist's is usually securely locked – a sad indictment of the age in which we live – but, should the 800-year-old church be unlocked, there is much of interest to attract the visitor. Of particular note are the effigies of two knights, one dating from the 14th century, unusually carved in wood, the other dating from the 13th century, carved in stone, the knight nearly swamped by his shield. It is believed that the knights were former lords of the local manor.

**Sodbury Fort** is a rectangular hillfort enclosing some 11 acres, whose origins can be traced back as far as the Iron Age. The scarp slope of the Cotswolds provided a natural defence on its western side, the remaining defences being double ramparts, an awesome 12 feet in height. The Romans strengthened and used the camp as one of their frontier posts, whilst in AD 577 the Saxon army camped here before the fateful battle at nearby Dyrham. In 1471 Edward IV rested here before moving on to destroy the army of Margaret of Anjou at the Battle of Tewkesbury. It is indeed a site of multi-occupancy, whose ancient fortifications hide many a tale of brave warriors past.

# Slaughterford and the By Brook Valley

## Down by the Riverside

*Many trout have their home in the By Brook.*

Slaughterford is a tiny hamlet deep in the By Brook Valley. Being in the heart of the Southern Cotswolds, every building is of stone, the golden limestone for which the region is so famous. The area boasts an isolated church, a scattering of farms, a few cottages and the occasional rather grand house, and little more. Without a main road in sight or sound, Slaughterford is truly far from the madding crowd. The By Brook itself is arguably the most beautiful of the Bristol Avon's tributary streams. Its clear waters are home to a good number of trout, with the fishing rights being jealously guarded, whilst the surrounding meadows and wooded hillsides provide a range of habitats for several species of wildfowl. With the added attraction of a fine old hostelry in Ford, this is altogether a perfect short walk.

# Kiddiwalks near Bristol & Bath

◆◆◆*5*◆◆◆◆◆◆◆◆◆◆◆◆◆◆◆◆◆◆◆◆◆◆◆◆◆◆◆

**Getting there** *Initially make for the Cold Ashton roundabout, 5 miles east of Bristol on the A420 road to Chippenham and 5 miles north of Bath on the A46 road to Stroud. Continue along the A420 towards Chippenham for 6 miles to Ford where, alongside the main road opposite the church, there is a small layby.*

**Length of walk** 2 miles
**Time** Allow $1^1/_2$ hours for the walk.
**Terrain** With the exception of a short hill between Ford and Slaughterford, this walk is easy going throughout. The outward leg to Slaughterford follows lanes that are virtually traffic-free, with the return to Ford being through meadowland alongside the By Brook. Buggies

## ◆ Fun Things to See and Do ◆

**The By Brook flows through** Ford and Slaughterford on its way to join the Bristol Avon near Bath. There are plenty of trout to catch sight of in the clean and virtually unpolluted river, basking in the sparkling waters. The river also attracts a wide range of water birds including kingfishers and herons, dippers and moorhens, whilst the surrounding meadows and woodland are home to raptors such as the buzzard and kestrel, as well as the occasional tawny and barn owl. It is always worth taking a pair of binoculars and a book of British birds on these walks and this particular one should provide plenty of variety to keep the younger ones interested. In summer make sure you take along some towels, so that the youngsters can enjoy a cool paddle at the point where the walk first joins the river. Here there are one or two shallows that are just perfect for small feet! Incidentally, as you walk down the track from Slaughterford to the By Brook, look out for a vast waterwheel in the bushes on your right. In years gone by, this provided the power for a local rag mill.

# Slaughterford and the By Brook Valley

would have to be carried across the fields ... although very young children would enjoy following the By Brook upstream.

**Start/Parking** A layby on the A420 Chippenham to Bristol road, opposite Ford church (GR 841749).

**Maps** OS Landranger 173 or OS Explorer 156.

**Refreshments** At journey's end, the White Hart Inn at Ford offers welcome rest and refreshment in a setting alongside the By Brook. Children are welcome in the restaurant area.

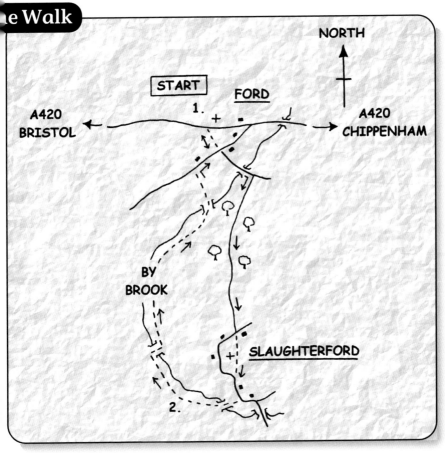

# Kiddiwalks near Bristol & Bath

◆ ◆ ◆ *5* ◆ ◆ ◆ ◆ ◆ ◆ ◆ ◆ ◆ ◆ ◆ ◆ ◆ ◆ ◆ ◆ ◆ ◆ ◆ ◆ ◆ ◆ ◆ ◆ ◆ ◆ ◆

❶ Walk to the Bristol end of the layby and turn left down a stepped path to emerge by the White Hart Inn in Ford. Cross over and follow the lane opposite that runs alongside the inn. Cross the By Brook and, in 30 yards, turn right along a quiet side lane. Follow this lane for 600 yards as it climbs uphill through Common Hill Plantation before dropping down to a junction on the edge of Slaughterford. Go over the stile opposite into a field in which stands Slaughterford church. Cross this field, passing to the left of the church, to a gate in the opposite field boundary. Follow the raised pavement ahead through Slaughterford and, where the road bears left, turn right through a gateway and follow a footpath through woodland down to footbridges over the By Brook.

❷ Cross these bridges and follow the river ahead upstream to a footbridge and sluices. Turn right, cross the river and turn left to follow the By Brook upstream. Aim for a stile in the far right corner of the first riverside meadow before making for the next stile on the far side of the

*This old waterwheel once provided the power for the local mill.*

# Slaughterford and the By Brook Valley

second meadow, the By Brook still flowing along on the left. In the following field, aim for a footbridge and sluices in the far right corner before following the river upstream for 75 yards. Just past the second of two seats on the riverbank, bear left away from the river to a gate in the corner of the field. Join the Colerne to Ford road, turn right and continue for 200 yards to the White Hart. The road can be relatively busy so exercise due care and attention. Turn left opposite the inn back up the stepped path to the A420 and the layby.

## Background Notes ◆

**Ford** lies on the busy A420 which prior to the coming of the M4 motorway was the main road from London to Bristol. Even before the invention of the internal combustion engine, the village lay on a coach route to Bristol, with today's OS Explorer maps still showing the 'Old Coach Road' running to the north of Ford. As with all coach stops, there had to be a coaching inn ... in this case, the White Hart. Sitting alongside the By Brook, the White Hart is one of the more popular destinations for residents of Bath and Bristol seeking a fine country hostelry. With heavy black beams and an ancient fireplace inscribed with the date 1553, the White Hart exudes a genuine sense of history. It also serves rather fine food and a selection of excellent real ales that might include Oakhill Best and Hop Back GFB.

**Slaughterford** is a beautiful place, primarily because of its location. Steep hillsides surround this small settlement, where the By Brook's waters were at one time harnessed to power local mills. Both a rag mill and a paper mill have provided employment here over the years, although today's visitor will be more impressed with the handsome stone cottages and houses. The church of St Nicholas is a most delightful building which had lain in ruinous decay for 200 years, having been ransacked by Cromwell's men, but was rebuilt and reopened in 1823. It stands in the middle of pastureland which is regularly grazed by cows. One local guidebook declares it to be 'so devoid of interest as to be worth a visit' – somewhat harsh criticism!

# 6

# Conham and the River Avon

## Ferry Boat Ride

Old maps of Conham – on the eastern fringes of Bristol – would not suggest promising walking country. The 1913 map, for example, shows a colliery and tramway, whilst the 1949 map shows a vast sewage works! Over the last 30 years, however, the worst excesses of the former industrial era have been eradicated, and the area bordering the River Avon has been transformed into the Conham River Park. Woodland and scrub now cover the former mineral workings, and a veritable wildlife haven has been created alongside the Avon. Across the river from Conham is Beese's Tea Gardens, with the small problem of crossing the water to find refreshment being solved by the presence of a seasonal weekend ferry – something that is bound to delight the younger members of your party.

# Conham and the River Avon

**Getting there** *Leave the A431 at a roundabout just west of Hanham's High Street and follow the road signposted to Conham. In 150 yards, turn right into Church Road and continue for 3/4 mile to a sharp right-hand bend. Immediately past this bend, turn left into the Conham River Park car park.*

**Length of walk** 1 mile
**Time** Allow at least 1 hour
**Terrain** As this is such a short walk it is suitable for even the youngest of toddlers, although they may need a helping hand on the steep path from the former copper smelter down to the River Avon.
**Start** The Conham River Park car park (GR 629722).

## Fun Things to See and Do ◆

**The Conham River Park** is an ideal place for a nature trail. Whether it is buddleia bushes, when in flower, that attract butterflies such as the peacock or red admiral, or the fungi that flourish in the damp woodland, there is something to spot at every turn throughout the year. Along the riverbank, there are birds in abundance. Swans and ducks, herons and coots are the most common species, and the sharp-eyed may even catch a glimpse of a kingfisher, whose blue and orange features are unmistakable. Water voles also live along the water's edge, although you will have to sit still and quietly to have a real chance of spotting one of these creatures on its travels!

Children will particularly enjoy ringing the bell to summon the ferry, which takes you across the River Avon from Conham to Beese's Tea Gardens, where you can enjoy a soft drink or an ice cream. The ferry, the last such service that now crosses the Avon along its length, only runs at weekends from Easter until early September, so be sure to time your visit to the Conham River Park to take advantage of this tea-time treat.

# Kiddiwalks near Bristol & Bath

♦♦♦**6**♦♦♦♦♦♦♦♦♦♦♦♦♦♦♦♦♦♦♦♦♦♦

**Maps** OS Landranger 172 or OS Explorer 155.

**Refreshments** Beese's Tea Gardens lie across the River Avon from Conham and they operate a ferry service across the river. Ring the bell on the Conham side to attract the ferryman's attention. Telephone 01179 77412 for details of opening times or visit their website at www.beeses.co.uk

## The Walk

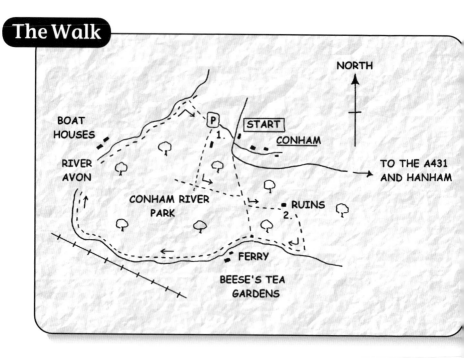

❶ Walk back towards the road from the car park but, rather than turning left to join the road, follow the footpath ahead, a single-storey building housing a rifle range to the left. Continue along this path for 150 yards until it emerges from scrubland onto a more open grassy hilltop. Turn left and follow a path for 120 yards to join Ferry Lane, a quiet woodland byway. Turn right and, in 30 yards, pass through a gap in an old wall on the left and continue

# Conham and the River Avon

along a path to some ruinous buildings that mark the site of a former copper smelter.

**❷** Immediately past these ruins, turn right and follow a rough steep path down to the River Avon. Turn right, and follow the riverbank for 125 yards to the bell and ferry crossing to Beese's Tea Gardens. Ferry Lane joins the riverbank at this point. Continue following the riverbank for $1/2$ mile until the car park comes into view on the right.

# Kiddiwalks near Bristol & Bath

## ◆ Background Notes ◆

**Conham** was for several centuries a heavily developed area bordering the River Avon. In 1937, a vast sewage works was built on part of the site occupied by the Conham River Park. The complex served the southern part of Kingswood until a trunk sewer was extended to Avonmouth. The site later became a refuse tip! All of this land originally belonged to Conham Hall, which was demolished in 1971. This stately home was associated with 17th-century non-conformism. Persecution forced the early Baptists to hold their meetings in secret in the local woodland and, in the period from 1680 to 1685, when the Bristol chapels were closed, the Hall became a haven for the local congregations. They would use the ferry to cross the Avon. Sadly, one of the boats sank in 1683, with a number of Baptists being drowned.

The ruined buildings in the woodland above the River Avon mark the site of a **copper smelter** set up in 1696. This was one of the first smelters to use coal – mined locally – rather than charcoal, making the process altogether more efficient. Subsequently, the buildings housed a small chemical works that processed animal waste products! Records also suggest that tallow candles were produced here for the local coal mines. The mines hereabouts were free of gas so naked lights could be used underground. The site – immediately above the navigable River Avon – was perfect insofar as the river provided water supply, power and transport.

Across the river at one point is a series of arches that carry Isambard Kingdom Brunel's **Great Western Railway** on its journey west from London to Bristol. 'God's Wonderful Railway' was opened on 31st August 1840. The arches were the scene of an act of great bravery in 1876. A local memorial tablet records how John Chiddy was killed by an express train when removing a large stone from the tracks of the railway. His actions saved many lives, but left his wife a widow and his family destitute.

# Willsbridge Mill and the Avon Valley Railway

## Trailing Trains and Nature Trails

*Along the way*

**M**any walkers looking for a stroll in the great outdoors would not give the Willsbridge region even a cursory glance. With sprawling housing estates and busy roads the area is very much indicative of East Bristol's rapid growth. Tucked away in this suburban sprawl, however, is a veritable oasis – the Willsbridge Valley – dissected by the Siston Brook. As well as exploring the nature trail in and around the valley, this walk includes the headquarters of the Avon Valley Railway. With working steam engines, a fully renovated Midland Railway station and a bustling and active network of sidings, the Avon Valley Railway provides a real trip down memory lane.

# Kiddiwalks near Bristol & Bath

**Getting there** *Bitton Station lies alongside the A431 midway between Bath and Bristol, approximately 1 mile north of Keynsham.*

**Distance** 1³/₄ miles
**Time** Allow up to 1¹/₂ hours for the walk.

**Terrain** This walk, being both short and generally level, is suitable for younger children. Half of the route provides easy going for buggies, although there are one or two narrow and rough sections of path.

## ◆ Fun Things to See and Do ◆

**Bitton Station** and the adjoining railway lines have been lovingly restored to bring the sights and sounds of the steam age back to the Avon Valley. At Christmas, 'Santa Specials' run on the line, whilst occasional 'Thomas the Tank Engine' weekends prove to be ever popular! In the sidings stand a number of static railway carriages. One is set aside for 'Bitton Bargains' – an Aladdin's Cave of bric-à-brac – whilst another is home to 'Bitton Bears' – a group of travelling teddy-bears that somehow got left behind when Santa visited the railway one Christmas past. The bears are quite happy in their carriage, and are used to children tapping on the window and pulling inquisitive faces at them!

**The Willsbridge Mill Reserve** contains a number of fascinating wildlife sites. The ponds, for example, provide homes for water boatmen and dragonflies, whilst along Siston Brook you might be able to point out the flash of a kingfisher or a dipper. Catscliffe Wood is home to bats, owls, jays, squirrels, foxes and badgers, whilst the traditional meadow is ablaze with butterflies during the summer. Throughout the year, special events are held at the mill, details of which can be found on the Avon Wildlife Trust's website: www.avonwildlifetrust.org.uk

# Willsbridge Mill and the Avon Valley Railway

◆◆◆◆◆◆◆◆◆◆◆◆◆◆◆◆◆◆◆◆◆◆◆◆◆◆◆◆◆◆

**Start/Parking** Bitton Station on the Avon Valley Railway (GR 670703).
**Maps** OS Landranger 172 or OS Explorer 155.
**Refreshments** The former waiting room at Bitton Station is now a buffet, offering hot food, drinks, ices and what the promotional literature describes as a range of 'legendary home-made cakes'. There are also picnic areas either side of the station building where packed meals can be enjoyed on warm days.

## The Walk

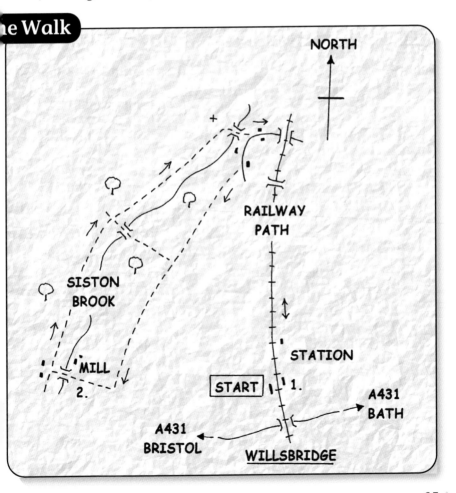

# Kiddiwalks near Bristol & Bath

**7**

● From the station, follow the Railway Path in a northerly direction for 600 yards to a bridge that carries Cherry Gardens Lane over the railway. Initially, the Railway Path passes the sidings complex on the left-hand side. Continue for 200 yards beyond this bridge, before bearing left through an exit point from the Railway Path, then bearing right down some steps to a back lane. Follow this lane downhill to the left, keeping on it as it bears left to then climb uphill to some 'blocking' bollards. Just beyond these bollards, turn right through a handgate and follow a path down to a stile just a few yards ahead. Turn left at this point and follow the path running above Siston Brook for 150 yards to a junction, where a path goes off on the right. Continue ahead along the path above the river for 400 yards to a stile and the Willsbridge Mill complex.

● Beyond the mill and education centre, turn right up an access lane to a junction in front of a property. Turn right and follow the path above the Siston Brook to a junction in 450 yards. Pass through the gateway opposite, and continue through the valley

# Willsbridge Mill and the Avon Valley Railway

## Background Notes ◆

**The Midland Railway** from Mangotsfield – through Bitton – to Bath Green Park received Parliamentary approval in July 1864. With work completed, including what the *Bath Chronicle* recorded as 'engineering features of considerable interest ... and cuttings ... long and deep', the line was officially opened on Wednesday 4th August 1869. Bitton Station, built out of the local stone and formed of two pavilions, employed in its heyday not only a station master and a porter, but also a porter/signalman, a junior porter, two further signalmen, clerks and junior clerks, with the latter being on just 8s 9d a week. The adjoining goods yard was a hive of activity, dispatching paper to London from a local mill as well as local flowers and vegetables to markets in Bristol. The line fell victim to the Beeching cuts of the 1960s, with the track finally being lifted in 1972. A preservation group was established that year with the aim of 'preserving, operating and exhibiting railway transportation systems for the public benefit'. Currently, the line is operating northwards as far as Oldland Common and in a southerly direction to the Rivers Boyd and Avon, with steam traction running regularly during the spring and summer months.

**Willsbridge Mill** is the main education and visitor centre for the Avon Wildlife Trust. The restored 19th-century corn mill, with its adjoining barn, is set in a 22-acre nature reserve that borders Siston Brook, a tributary of the Bristol Avon. The nature reserve has a variety of habitats, including meadow and woodland, ponds and streams, as well as a wildlife garden where the aim is to show visitors how their own gardens can be made more appealing to wildlife. In the valley behind Willsbridge Mill is evidence of the area's industrial past. Exposed rock faces remain from when pennant sandstone was quarried from the valley's sides, whilst the valley floor carries the remains of the 'Dramway', a historic mineral railway. In the 19th century, horse-drawn trucks came along the Dramway from the Bristol Coalfield around Coalpit Heath and Pucklechurch, carrying coal down to barges on the River Avon at Keynsham.

to a gate below St Anne's church in 150 yards. Turn right over a footbridge to a junction and follow the road around to the left for 100 yards to steps on the right leading up to the Railway Path. Climb these steps, then turn left to reach the Railway Path before turning right to retrace your steps to Bitton Station.

# 8

# Saltford, the River Avon and the Railway Path

## Boats and Trains

A local railway preservation group, who run regular weekend and Bank Holiday steam excursions, is slowly restoring the former Midland Railway from Bristol to Bath. Alongside the tracks runs the 'Bristol & Bath Railway Path', which will enable youngsters to enjoy the sites and sounds of a bygone era. Away from the Railway Path, the walk follows a navigable stretch of the River Avon, with any number of pleasure craft making their way between Bath and Bristol. Towards journey's end, the route passes the Jolly Sailor Inn sitting proudly on the riverbank at Saltford. Dating from the 18th century, this was originally a watering hole for bargees. Today, it is simply a place to rest awhile and watch the boats tackling the adjoining lock.

# Saltford, the River Avon and the Railway Path

## Fun Things to See and Do ◆

**As you walk along the Railway Path,** you will come across an exposed section of rock alongside the track bed. These rocks, cleared by the Bristol City Museum, represent the floor of an ancient sea that covered the area over 200 million years ago. This was during a period of geological history called the 'Lower Jurassic Period' when the warm waters would have been home to such ancient creatures as ammonites, benomnites and grypphae. Over the years, pressure turned the muddy sediments on the seabed into the rocks we see today, whilst the remains of the sea creatures were preserved as fossils. A woodland has recently been created alongside Swineford Lock. Known as '**Saltford Community Forest**', its $3^1/_2$ acres contain over 1,000 trees and 375 shrubs. The trees include ash and wild cherry, oak and lime, whilst the shrubs include dogwood and guelder rose, hazel and dog rose – great fun for hiding behind, before springing out on the 'unsuspecting' adult. See how many species the children can identify! The woodland, lying alongside the River Avon, provides a perfect picnic spot. Any leftover pieces of bread or cake can be fed to the ducks and other wildfowl that make this stretch of the river their home.

# Kiddiwalks near Bristol & Bath

◆ ◆ ◆ *8* ◆ ◆ ◆ ◆ ◆ ◆ ◆ ◆ ◆ ◆ ◆ ◆ ◆ ◆ ◆ ◆ ◆ ◆ ◆ ◆ ◆ ◆

this walk, is excellent for pushchairs and buggies. The riverside section of the path, however, follows fieldpaths which are less easy to negotiate.
**Start/Parking** The Railway Path in Saltford (GR 688675).

**Maps** OS Landranger 172 or OS Explorer 155.
**Refreshments** Both the Bird in Hand and Jolly Sailor pubs are excellent, family-friendly hostelries. The Jolly Sailor enjoys a marvellous riverside location.

## The Walk

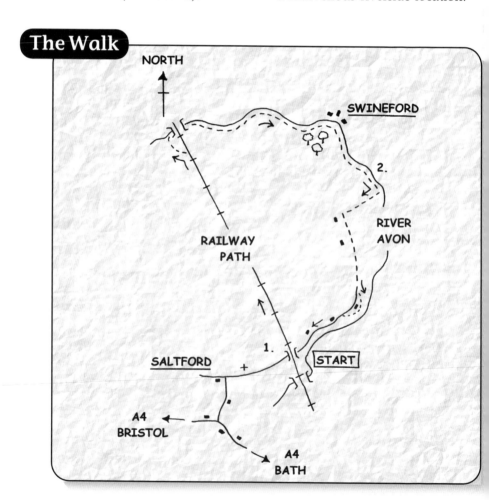

# Saltford, the River Avon and the Railway Path

◆◆◆◆◆◆◆◆◆◆◆◆◆◆◆◆◆◆◆◆◆◆◆◆◆◆◆◆◆◆◆◆

**❶** Walk back to the railway bridge and, just before the bridge itself, follow the path on the left that slopes gently uphill to join the Railway Path. Turn right, and continue on the Railway Path for ³/₄ mile. Just before a bridge over the Avon, cross a stile on the left, turn right and follow the edge of a field down to the riverbank. Turn right, pass under the bridge and enter a riverside field. Follow the left edges of five fields alongside the river upstream to a stile in ¹/₂ mile just by Swineford Lock. Cross the stile, and enter a part of Saltford Community Forest. Cross to a stile ahead, walk through the

enclosure containing Swineford Lock and continue to a stile in the fence on the right.

**❷** Turn left, and continue following the river upstream – through an enclosure by a slipway – and onto the corner of a field where the path turns right. Follow a grassy ride ahead for 300 yards up to a waterboard complex, walking away from the Avon. On reaching the complex, walk along a short section of enclosed path to a stile on the left before following the right edge of the field ahead to a gateway. Then continue on a grassy track through to a stile and

# Kiddiwalks near Bristol & Bath

the lane by the Jolly Sailor Inn. Turn left through the pub car park to the river, then turn right and follow the riverside path past the Jolly Sailor and through to the road. Turn left and follow the road for 400 yards back to the parking area, all the while bordering the river.

## ◆ Background Notes ◆

**The Railway Path utilises the trackbed** of the former Midland Railway that ran from Bristol Temple Meads out through Mangotsfield and on to Green Park Station in Bath, now better known as the site of the local Sainsbury's supermarket. Closed by Beeching in the 1960s, the old line was turned into one of the country's first cycle/walkways by the local council. At the former Bitton Station, the Bristol Suburban Railway Society have their base, with locomotives in steam on many weekends during the year as well as on Bank Holidays. The railway has currently been restored as far as the point where the walk joins the River Avon and so, timetables permitting, you may catch a glimpse of the former glories of the steam age.

Being elevated above the surrounding countryside, the views from the old line are particularly good. On the left lies the Avon Vale, surrounded by flat agricultural land with the Mendip Hills rising in the distance, whilst on the right are the hills above Bitton and Swineford, with Upton Cheyney and North Stoke nestling on their slopes. Especially prominent is Kelston Round Hill, topped with a clump of trees that are a landmark from so many places in the Bath and Bristol region.

**The Avon Navigation** between Bristol and Bath was given Parliamentary assent in 1712 and, by 1727, the six locks that overcome the rise of some 30 feet between the two cities were constructed. There had always been trade along the river, but this had been hindered by both droughts and the many shallows due to the river's mills. This walk passes the locks at both Swineford and Saltford, which are today alive with the sounds of pleasure craft. It was not always this way, however. The opening of the navigation saw large volumes of Shropshire coal arriving in the area by way of the River Severn. The local miners, seeing the threat this posed to their own livelihoods, took the law into their own hands, destroying the lock at Saltford, for example. None of the culprits were apprehended, which was probably as well with 'damaging the navigation' being an offence that carried the death penalty.

# Northend and Solsbury Hill

*Where Kestrels Fly*

*Chilcombe Bottom*

P opular music fans in their late 30s and 40s will remember Solsbury Hill as being the influence for a song of that name that reached number 13 in the charts in 1977 for Peter Gabriel, former frontman with the rock band Genesis. The lyrics talk of time standing still as an 'eagle flew out of the night'. Although you will never see eagles around Solsbury Hill, you might well spot a buzzard or kestrel hovering over the lower slopes of the hillside in search of its prey. Hidden away in Chilcombe Bottom below Solsbury Hill is an erstwhile reservoir that has now been transformed into a nature reserve. This wetland is home to a variety of water-loving flora and fauna, including several species of duck.

# Kiddiwalks near Bristol & Bath

◆ ◆ ◆*9*◆ ◆ ◆ ◆ ◆ ◆ ◆ ◆ ◆ ◆ ◆ ◆ ◆ ◆ ◆ ◆ ◆ ◆ ◆ ◆ ◆ ◆ ◆ ◆ ◆ ◆

**Getting there** *From the large roundabout on the eastern edge of Bath where the A46 meets the A4, follow the London Road into Batheaston village. In the centre of the village, follow the minor road signposted to Northend and St Catherine's to reach the Northend Inn.*

**Length of walk** 3 miles

**Time** Allow at least 2 hours, given the climb onto Solsbury Hill.

**Terrain** With the stiff climb onto Solsbury Hill, this walk is better suited to slightly older children rather than toddlers. Quiet lanes and footpaths are followed to and from the summit of the hill. This, together with the gradients, makes it a difficult walk with buggies.

## ◆ Fun Things to See and Do ◆

**The steep climb onto Solsbury Hill** represents a real challenge for eager little legs. Although it appears to be pretty tough and demanding, the hilltop is actually little more than 640 feet above sea level. It might be useful here, by way of encouragement, to draw comparison with Snowdon, the highest mountain in England and Wales, which is nearly 3,000 feet higher! The sense of achievement once you have made it to the top is incalculable and the view from Solsbury Hill is pretty impressive. Among the landmarks to point out are Bath Abbey, the white horses at Westbury and Cherhill, and the Mendip Hills. Solsbury Hill is a rather fine vantage point and in centuries past, when invaders often attacked villages, settlements were usually built on these hilltops so that the enemy could be spotted on the move. The humps and bumps that surround the edges of Solsbury Hill are ancient ramparts, designed to keep out unwanted intruders. Challenge the children to try running up these ramparts to reach the hilltop while you unpack the picnic, a suitable reward for their efforts.

# Northend and Solsbury Hill

**Start/Parking** On the roadside in Northend between the Northend Inn and Eagle House (GR 779683).
**Maps** OS Landranger 172 or OS Explorer 155.

**Refreshments** Solsbury Hill is the perfect spot for a picnic. There is a local pub at the start of the walk – the Northend Inn – but it is not especially family-orientated.

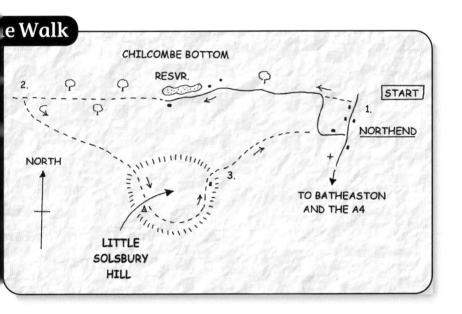

e Walk

CHILCOMBE BOTTOM

RESVR.

2.

START

1.

NORTHEND

NORTH

3.

TO BATHEASTON
AND THE A4

LITTLE
SOLSBURY
HILL

❶ Continue in a northerly direction from the Northend Inn for 200 yards to Eagle House. Immediately past Eagle House, turn left along a lane that soon becomes an unmetalled track. Follow this track for 250 yards to its junction with a quiet lane. Keep ahead along this lane, initially climbing uphill before dropping down into a valley where, in 600 yards, a stone outbuilding – similar to a lock-up – appears on the right-hand side of the road. Climb the steps to the right of this building to a gate, beyond which lies Chilcombe Reservoir. Return to the lane and continue for 150 yards to a detached property on the left. Beyond this cottage,

# Kiddiwalks near Bristol & Bath

follow an enclosed path through the valley bottom for 600 yards to reach a small stone barn on the left.

❷ Pass through a gateway on the left and head across a field, bearing slightly to the right and heading uphill away from the valley bottom. Continue past some ash trees, before climbing uphill to a stile. Turn left and follow the left edge of a field to the next stile, then walk along an enclosed path that climbs steadily to reach another stile. Continue uphill through the ramparts of a hillfort to reach the top of Solsbury

# Northend and Solsbury Hill

Hill. Turn right, and follow the edge of the hilltop around to a trig point with a fine view across Bath. Continue around the hilltop to a National Trust sign, and carry on walking to the north-eastern corner of the hilltop, where a cottage appears at the foot of the slope of the right.

**3** Drop down the bank to this cottage, and cross a stile in the hedgerow to the left of the property. Enter a hillside field, and head across the middle of this field to a stile in the opposite field boundary. Continue following the left edges of the next two fields and then the left edge of a market garden down to Seven Acre Lane in Northend. Drop downhill to the main road in the village, where a right turn brings you back to the Northend Inn.

## Background Notes ◆

**Batheaston was for many years** renowned for its notorious traffic jams. The main street through the village was the A4 – the London Road – one of the busiest thoroughfares leading into Bath. The recently constructed bypass may have raised the blood pressure of local environmentalists, but it has certainly brought a little more tranquillity into the lives of local residents. **Northend**, the starting point of the walk, is the oldest part of Batheaston. It is here that we find St Nicholas' church, a Victorian reconstruction, with a number of older elements that include the 15th-century tower and a font dating from 1700. Many fine old properties line the roadside in Northend including Eagle House, built by John Wood the Elder, one of the great architects of Georgian Bath.

**Solsbury Hill** provides a truly spectacular 360° panorama across the local landscape. From Bath to Salisbury Plain, from the Mendip Hills to the Wiltshire Downs, there are landmarks in every direction. Such a vantage point attracted the very earliest settlers. In the Iron Age, sometime between 300 and 100 BC, a walled village was developed on the hilltop. Initially, an area close to the hilltop was cleared to a rock base on which timber framed wattle huts were constructed. A 20 foot wide rampart was then built, faced inside and out with well-built drystone walls and infilled with loose stone. The outer face of this fortification was at least 12 feet high. The National Trust information panel records how, after a period of occupation, some of the huts were burned down and the rampart was overthrown. The site was abandoned and never occupied again.

# 10

# Brown's Folly Nature Reserve

## Towering Statement

O n a steep hillside above the Avon Valley east of Bath, former limestone quarries have been overtaken by nature. Limestone grassland, deciduous woodland and exposed rock faces make up this fine nature reserve, with Wade-Brown's 19th-century folly dominating the scene. As well as a rich flora and fauna, which includes both orchids and slow-worms, the reserve provides magnificent views that extend across the River Avon towards Solsbury Hill, Bathampton Down and the golden terraces of Bath itself.

# Brown's Folly Nature Reserve

**Getting there** *Follow the A363 from Bathford for 3 miles towards Bradford-on-Avon. At the top of Bathford Hill, turn left along the road signposted to Monkton Farleigh. In ¹/₂ mile, at a junction in the village, turn left and head out to Farleigh Rise. In ¹/₂ mile, just as this lane begins to drop downhill, turn left into the woodland car park.*

**Length of walk** 1³/₄ miles

**Time** Allow about 1¹/₂ hours for the walk.

**Terrain** A short walk, this route is suitable for children of all ages. The going underfoot is rough on occasions, so a steadying hand may be needed.

**Start/Parking** Brown's Folly Reserve car park (GR 798663).

**Maps** OS Landranger 172 or OS Explorer 155.

**Refreshments** The King's Arms in Monkton Farleigh is just ¹/₂ mile from the start of the walk.

## The Walk

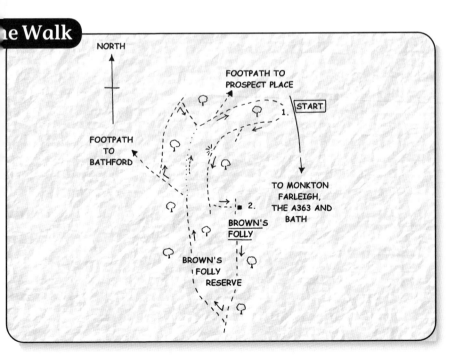

# Kiddiwalks near Bristol & Bath

**1** As you enter the car park, look out for a gap in the fence on the left. Pass through this gap, climb some steps to an information board and continue on into the woodland. In a few yards, climb a short flight of steps to join a main woodland path, turn right and follow what is waymarked as the 'Pepperbox Trail'. In 200 yards, ignore a path on the left, keeping ahead instead on the main path

## ◆ Fun Things to See and Do ◆

**Brown's Folly lends its name** to the local nature reserve, an area of mixed woodland, scrub and limestone grassland that has grown over the remains of the former stone quarries. As you walk around you will spot rock faces and boulders now overgrown with plants and shrubs. This provides an exciting backdrop for the imagination of the young as they scramble over rocks. Do be careful, however, as some parts are loose and unstable. The rich flora and fauna includes badgers, harebells, rockrose, woolly thistle and agrimony. You might also spot the occasional cave or rock shelter, although most of these have now been 'fenced off' to prevent the local bat population from being disturbed. But if you look carefully, there are still one or two open caves to explore.

The stone in the reserve is limestone, which was formed millions of years ago when a shallow sea covered this part of the world. Small sea-creatures would fall to the bottom of this sea and, over a period of time, the pressure would cause their bodies and shells to solidify into rock. If you look carefully at some broken pieces of limestone, it is possible to make out the fossilised remains of some ancient sea creature. On hot days, the exposed stone becomes a suntrap where lizards and slow-worms may occasionally appear. These creatures are quite harmless, but are very delicate, so do not encourage little fingers to pick them up.

# Brown's Folly Nature Reserve

emerges onto an open stretch of hillside with fine views across the Avon Valley towards Bath. Continue directly ahead across this open clearing and on downhill to reach a junction of paths. Follow the stepped path on the left uphill to reach Brown's Folly.

❷ Turn right on reaching the hilltop path by the folly, and follow what is the upper boundary wall of the reserve for 550 yards to a sharp right turn – there is another 'Pepperbox Trail' sign. Turn right, and follow a path for 350 yards until it emerges onto the foot of an open hillside, ignoring one left turn. Continue following the main path directly ahead for 1/2 mile back to the parking area, ignoring a couple of left turns as you go.

that runs across the north-facing slopes of the reserve. In 120 yards, keep on this path as it bears left to continue along the west-facing slopes of the hillside. Continue along this pathway until it

## Background Notes ◆

Brown's Folly stands proudly above a hillside that is riddled with miles of passages and tunnels. From this subterranean world came much of the golden limestone that was used as the building material for those remarkable Georgian terraces in nearby Bath. The folly itself was commissioned in 1849 by a Mr Wade-Brown, a local quarry owner, allegedly to promote the quality of his building stone. The quarrying business was at the time going through a downturn in its fortunes, and Wade-Brown saw the folly as a means of employing idle workers, as well as a grand advertisement for his wares.

# 11

# Bradford-on-Avon and Avoncliff

## Down by the Riverside

The Avon Valley south of Bath provides some of the most popular and best-loved walking destinations in the area. From Bradford-on-Avon, an ancient Saxon town that has been described as a 'clone of Bath', this walk follows the Kennet and Avon Canal to the neighbouring hamlet of Avoncliff. This is a thriving section of the canal, with barges and pleasure craft creating a lively and colourful scene. Having enjoyed a beer or a cream tea in Avoncliff, where the canal crosses the River Avon by means of a vast aqueduct, the river itself is followed back into Bradford-on-Avon. Heron and mallard, moorhen and coot are commonplace hereabouts, as are anglers seeking the elusive 'one that got away'. At journey's end in Bradford, a child's play area will allow youngsters to burn off any excess energy that still remains following this fine waterside walk.

# Bradford-on-Avon and Avoncliff

**Getting there** *Travelling southwards, follow the A363 Bath to Trowbridge road into the centre of Bradford-on-Avon. Having crossed the Town Bridge that carries the main road across the River Avon, continue for 100 yards to a roundabout where a right turn leads to the station. Bradford-on-Avon, incidentally, is served by a regular railway service from both Bath and Bristol.*

**Length of walk** 3 miles
**Time** Allow 2 hours for the walk
**Terrain** Other than a short

stepped path down to the River Avon in Avoncliff, this walk is suitable for buggies, with the riverside meadows being crossed by a firm grassy footpath that is regularly mowed. The rest of the walk follows tarmac paths or canal towpath, which buggies will have no problems negotiating.

**Start/Parking** The station car park in Bradford-on-Avon (GR 824607).

**Maps** OS Landranger 173 or OS Explorer 156.

**Refreshments** There are pubs and tea rooms in both Bradford-on-Avon and Avoncliff. The Cross

## Fun Things to See and Do ◆

**As you walk along the canal towpath**, you may well come across one of the waterborne travellers who make their living selling arts and crafts to passing visitors. It may be an artist, it could be a wood carver, it might even be a painter of those colourful jugs and pots that adorn so many barges. One thing that you will inevitably spot is a family of ducks – usually mallards – that make their home along the waterway; so make sure you have some old bread or stale cake to hand. Along the riverbank, keep your eyes open for kingfishers, several of which regularly frequent the Avon between Bradford and Avoncliff. Back in Bradford, take time to explore the ancient tithe barn. A tithe is a tenth and, in centuries past, farmers would have to give a tenth of their crops to the landowners. The grain and wheat was stored in these tithe barns.

# Kiddiwalks near Bristol & Bath

◆ ◆ ◆ *11* ◆ ◆ ◆ ◆ ◆ ◆ ◆ ◆ ◆ ◆ ◆ ◆ ◆ ◆ ◆ ◆ ◆ ◆ ◆ ◆ ◆ ◆ ◆ ◆ ◆

Guns at Avoncliff can boast a riverside terrace, whilst the Bridge Tea Rooms in Bradford has an enviable reputation due to its starring role in a soap powder commercial!

## The Walk

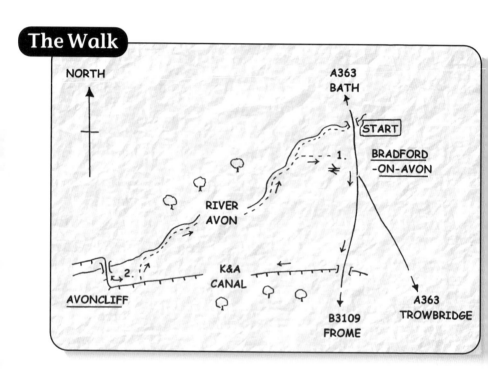

❶ From the station car park, return to the main road and turn right to follow the B3109, Frome Road, past the Three Horseshoes pub. In 400 yards, turn right by the Lock Inn to join the Kennet and Avon Canal. Follow the towpath for 1¼ miles into Avoncliff, where rest and refreshment can be enjoyed either at the Cross Guns pub or the Mad Hatter Tea Room. Retrace your steps back along the towpath for 100 yards to an information board and a stepped path on the left leading down to the River Avon.

❷ Descend the steps to the

riverbank, turn right and follow the Avon upstream across four fields. At the far side of the fourth field, pass through a gateway and follow a short track alongside the river before joining a tarmac path. Continue along this tarmac path, still bordering the river, until you reach a packhorse bridge on the left – to the right is Bradford's tithe barn. Follow the gravel path ahead across a grassy recreation area, pass under a railway bridge and follow the path to the right up into the station car park.

# Kiddiwalks near Bristol & Bath

## ◆ Background Notes ◆

**Bradford-on-Avon** is a former weaving town, with several of the old mills still dominating the town centre. Rows of weavers' cottages line the hillside above the river, all lovingly crafted from the local golden limestone. The town is a veritable paradise for lovers of fine architecture with the rich array of attractions including a vast tithe barn, a Saxon church, the Town Bridge with its ancient lock-up and the Shambles, a picturesque shopping street. One of the lesser-known attractions is the town's museum, housed above the library, which documents the history of Bradford using photographs, historical documents and artefacts. Bradford, incidentally, literally translates to 'broad ford', a reference to a crossing point over the river that lay alongside the Town Bridge.

**The Kennet and Avon Canal:** The River Kennet between Newbury and Reading had been navigable since the early 18th century, as had the Avon Navigation between Bath and Bristol. All that remained was to bridge the gap between Bath and Newbury, a mere 57 miles, and London would have a direct link with Bristol. By 1810, work on Caen Hill in Devizes was completed and the *Bath Herald* was able to report that 'the guns were fired on Sydney Wharf' alongside the canal's headquarters in Cleveland House. Traffic on the canal followed an all too familiar pattern. There was an initial boom – the K&A carried 341,878 tons of freight in 1838, for example, with the main cargo being coal from the Somerset Coalfield around Radstock. Once the Great Western Railway was opened, the inevitable decline set in and the canal fell into disrepair. Recent years have seen the complete restoration of the waterway, culminating in its official reopening by the Queen in August 1990.

**Avoncliff** is an isolated hamlet tucked away in one of the least accessible corners of the Avon Valley. Dominating the settlement is the 110 yard long aqueduct that carries the K&A across the River Avon itself. Constructed of the local Bath stone, its essential features are three arches, a solid parapet and balustraded ends. Stone quarries were once worked at Westwood on the hilltops above Avoncliff, with a tramline running down the hillside from the stone workings to the canal. The weir upstream of the aqueduct originally powered two flock mills. The dereliction of the left-hand mill is in marked contrast to the handsome conversion that has turned its partner into a fine residence.

# 2

# *Wellow and Stony Littleton Long Barrow*

## Underground, Overground

*Stony Littleton Long Barrow*

The village of Wellow, just a few miles south of Bath, clings to a south-facing hillside above the Wellow Brook. It really is an enviable location, with an outlook that extends across the rolling hills of North Somerset. The walk initially follows the meadowland bordering the Wellow Brook, a waterside stroll that is surrounded by an abundance of moisture-loving flora and fauna. On the hilltop above the river stands Stony Littleton Long Barrow. Dating from 2000 BC, this chambered burial tomb is a fascinating monument to explore – both inside and out! A secluded green lane descends the hillside back to the river, where you can splash your way through a shallow ford or keep your feet dry by crossing an ancient packhorse bridge. A short climb up the hillside back into Wellow brings you to the Fox and Badger Inn and journey's end, welcome rest and refreshment following a delightful stroll through the Somerset countryside.

# Kiddiwalks near Bristol & Bath

*12*

**Getting there** *Follow the A367 road south from Bath to Peasedown St John before heading east on the unclassified road signposted to Wellow. It is just 2 miles to the centre of the village and the Fox and Badger pub.*

**Length of walk** 2½ miles
**Time** Allow 2 hours for the walk and exploring Stony Littleton Long Barrow.
**Terrain** With most of the walk following fieldpaths and tracks, it is unsuitable for buggies and pushchairs. Very young children might therefore appreciate the odd piggyback! There is one climb uphill to Stony Littleton Long Barrow, but it is a short and relatively gentle ascent.
**Start/Parking** The village square in Wellow in the vicinity of the Fox and Badger (GR 740583).
**Maps** OS Landranger 172 or OS Explorer 142.
**Refreshments** The Fox and Badger at Wellow will offer welcome rest and respite at journey's end. The grassy area around Stony Littleton Long Barrow is an excellent picnic spot.

## ◆ Fun Things to See and Do ◆

**The first part of the walk** alongside this tributary stream of the Bristol Avon is home to a good number of trout, whilst kingfisher and moorhen, coot and mallard are often seen in and around the water. Towards journey's end, a shallow ford takes a quiet lane through the river. The water is shallow enough to paddle safely here, and it is also a good place to catch a few minnows and other small creatures that lurk therein. On the hilltop above the river is an **ancient burial chamber** where local farmers and their families were buried thousands of years ago, so be sure to take a torch with you so that the interior of this long barrow can be explored. Alternatively, if you do not fancy entering this ancient tomb, simply rest on top of the grassy mound and enjoy the fine views across towards Wellow.

# Wellow and Stony Littleton Long Barrow

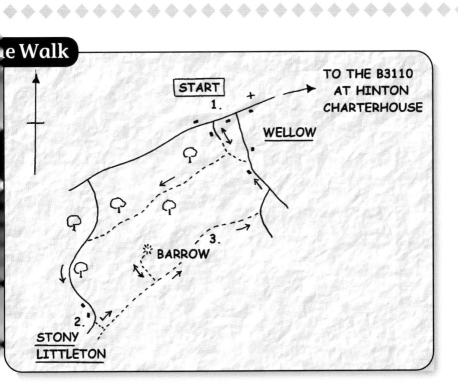

① Follow the back lane down past the Fox and Badger to the former trackbed of the Somerset & Dorset Railway. Pass through a gateway opposite, to the right of the former signal box, and continue downhill on a footpath for 120 yards. Opposite a cottage on the left, turn right along a path to a stile. Walk the whole length of the field ahead to a stile at its far end, before passing through a small area of woodland into the next field. Walk the whole length of this field to the next stile, then enter a large riverside meadow.

Follow the Wellow Brook for 600 yards to a stile and lane at the far side of the meadow. Turn left along this lane, and continue for 500 yards to a property called 'Greenacres'.

② Turn left, cross the Wellow Brook and then go left again to a stile. Follow the hedge on the left uphill for 150 yards, before leaving the main path to detour to Stony Littleton Long Barrow. This involves crossing a stile on the left and following a hedge across a hillside field for 200 yards to a stile

# Kiddiwalks near Bristol & Bath

on the right. Cross this stile and ahead is the barrow. Retrace your steps back to the main path, and turn left to a gate to the top of the hill. Beyond this gate, follow a hedge on the right across the hilltop and, where the hedge ends, continue across the open hilltop to a gate in the end field boundary.

Continue along a track for 500 yards to a lane, before keeping ahead to a junction. Turn left down to the ford, cross the packhorse bridge and follow the gravelled path ahead uphill to the signal box and the lane leading back to the Fox and Badger.

## ◆ Background Notes ◆

**Wellow** is a picturesque hillside village, whose southerly aspect makes it all the more attractive when its handsome houses are picked out by the rays of the setting sun. Rising above the village is the splendid tower of St Julian's church, constructed – quite naturally for these parts – in the Somerset Perpendicular style. Wellow is centred around a village square, where a working farm and ranks of stone cottages sit cheek by jowl with the Fox and Badger, a popular traditional country inn. The Somerset & Dorset Railway, that most noted of the Beeching cuts of 1966, ran through the village. Abbreviated to simply the 'S&D', it was the 'swift and delightful' to some, the 'slow and dirty' to others. The former signal box is passed just below the Fox and Badger, a familiar sight to the passengers who used the railway to travel south from Bath to Radstock, Shepton Mallet and ultimately Bournemouth.

**Stony Littleton Long Barrow** is a Neolithic tomb used for collective burial and dating back to 2000 BC. A plaque at its entrance boasts that 'this tumulus is declared by competent judges to be the most perfect specimen of Celtic Antiquity still existing in Great Britain' – it is hard to disagree. It evidently became 'much injured' due to the 'lapse of time or the carelessness of its former proprietors' but was 'restored in 1858 with scrupulous exactness'. It is possible to enter the barrow to a depth of 50 feet from the entrance and to examine the three pairs of burial chambers that lie either side of the central gallery.

# 3

# *Litton Lakes*

*Water, Water, Everywhere*

Litton Upper Lake, one of two small reservoirs in the East Mendips

W hen Bristolians refer to their 'Lake District' they invariably are talking about the Chew Valley with its massive reservoirs – Blagdon Lake and Chew Valley Lake itself. Less well-known are the Litton Lakes, a pair of diminutive reservoirs tucked into a fold of the East Mendip landscape. As well as being a haven for wildfowl, part of the upper reservoir is a breeding ground for the trout that are used to stock the nearby Chew Valley Lake.

# Kiddiwalks near Bristol & Bath

**13**

### Getting there

*Follow the A39 to Chewton Mendip, and turn left on the B3114 to Litton. Pass the Kings Arms and take the second of these turnings – Back Lane – before turning right at the next junction in 300 yards. Continue for 200 yards, and park by the entrance to a waterboard installation, being careful not to block the access gateway.*

**Length of walk** 2 miles
**Time** Allow up to 2 hours
**Terrain** The footpaths and access roads that follow the northern banks of the lakes would be suitable for sturdy buggies. The circuit of the lower reservoir, however, follows field paths and narrow waterside paths that are not suitable for buggies or pushchairs.

## The Walk

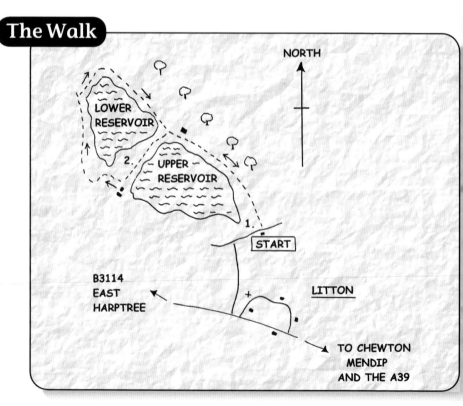

NORTH

LOWER
RESERVOIR

2. UPPER
RESERVOIR

1.

START

B3114
EAST
HARPTREE

LITTON

TO CHEWTON
MENDIP
AND THE A39

# Litton Lakes

◆◆◆◆◆◆◆◆◆◆◆◆◆◆◆◆◆◆◆◆◆◆◆◆◆◆◆◆◆◆

**Start/Parking** The quiet lane north of Litton giving access to the upper reservoir (GR 595549). **Maps** OS Landranger 171 or OS Explorer 141. **Refreshments** The Kings Arms in Litton is a centuries-old hostelry that has earned a fine reputation for both its food and drinks selection. There is also a children's play area outside the inn, which makes this an ideal venue for family groups.

## Fun Things to See and Do ◆

**Litton Lakes** – and the surrounding woodland – provide a number of habitats that attract a rich variety of wildlife. The peaceful waters of the reservoirs are home to plenty of birds, including coot and moorhen, swan and mallard, tufted duck and heron, so yet again have a pair of binoculars at the ready, as well as a bird spotting guide, to see just how many different species you can identify. Foxes and badgers, reed warblers and pied wagtails, peacock and tortoiseshell butterflies also live here and provide a veritable naturalist's paradise.

You might notice that a section of the lower reservoir – immediately below the upper dam – is cordoned off with a net. Look carefully, and you will spot fish jumping up out of the water at this point. This part of the lake is used to breed trout that are then taken to the Chew Valley Reservoir to stock what is one of the best trout fisheries in the country. Youngsters – as well as adults – will marvel as these game fish quite literally jump high above the water's surface in their quest for flies and other small creatures. The reason for the net is quite simple – it is to prevent the local wildfowl swooping on the lake and eating these carefully bred and valuable fish.

❶ Pass through the gateway opposite the waterboard installation and follow the path to the right that soon borders the narrow tapered end of the upper reservoir. Follow the path beside the water's edge for $1/2$ mile down to the dam at the bottom end of the upper reservoir. Turn left and, on the far side of the dam, cross the footbridge over an overflow channel before continuing down the path on the right to reach the lower reservoir. Walk on the footpath around the southern edge of this lower lake for 200 yards, then follow a stream ahead along to a stile. Cross another stile ahead, and continue for 40 yards towards some properties.

❷ At this point, cross a footbridge on the right over the stream before crossing a stile into a field. Follow the perimeter of this field to the right, around to the far right corner of the field. Cross a stile at this point, and follow the right edge of the following field to a gate in its corner. Beyond this gate, turn right over a cattle grid to reach the dam at the foot of the lower reservoir. On the far side of this dam, turn right and follow a tarmac access road for 350 yards alongside the lower reservoir, before continuing uphill to a cottage on the left and the upper dam. Follow the path ahead alongside the left-hand edge of the reservoir, retracing your steps back to the lane and parking area.

## ◆ Background Notes ◆

**Litton Lakes:** The reservoirs at Litton were constructed by Irish navvies in the mid-19th century. The lower reservoir was completed in 1846, followed by the upper reservoir just four years later. At the time, Catholicism was not widely practised in this corner of Somerset, and the migrant labourers caused something of a stir when mass was said in Litton church. There are also historic accounts of the navvies kneeling in the mud around the mill at nearby Sherborne Farm in Litton village whilst practising their faith.

These stretches of water were constructed as 'compensation reservoirs' by the damming of the River Chew. The source of the Chew is found at a number of springs a mile or so upstream near the village of Chewton Mendip, springs that the Bristol Waterworks Company used for its water supplies. The reservoirs prevented disruption for local residents when the springs were being drawn upon for supply purposes.

# 14

# Ebbor Gorge near Priddy

*Gorge Walking*

*A rocky outcrop above Ebbor Gorge*

This is a short but quite strenuous walk around Ebbor Gorge, a fine example of a Mendip valley. The walk does involve a scramble up through the gorge itself, which the youngsters will thoroughly enjoy but which is best left alone by elderly grandparents! Be aware that the viewpoint above the gorge is directly above vertical cliffs, so it is essential that a tight rein is kept on any little ones in your party. The outlook from this lofty hilltop perch is quite exceptional, extending across much of Central and West Somerset. The remainder of the walk follows shady and secluded woodland paths, through an area of ancient deciduous tree cover. With a picnic area alongside the car park, this will prove to be a fine family trip – an exciting and exhilarating walk followed by some well-deserved rest and refreshment.

# Kiddiwalks near Bristol & Bath

## *14*

**Getting there** *Ebbor Gorge and its parking area lie just off of the Wookey Hole to Priddy minor road. Wookey Hole, being a major national tourist attraction, is well signposted from Wells.*

**Length of walk** 2 miles
**Time** Allow about 1½ hours for the walk.

**Terrain** With stepped paths and a rocky scramble, this walk is totally unsuitable for buggies and pushchairs.
**Start/Parking** Ebbor Gorge car park (GR 520485).
**Maps** OS Landranger 182 or OS Explorer 141.
**Refreshments** There are no refreshment facilities on this walk, so pack a picnic to enjoy at the picnic site at Ebbor.

## The Walk

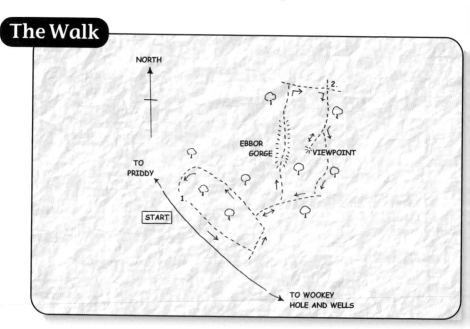

❶ Walk down to the bottom of the parking area, moving away from the information centre at the top of the site, and continue following the path down through the picnic area. Pass the National Trust viewpoint on the left, and continue along a grassy track downhill through the woodland to a clearing and a crosstrack. Turn

# Ebbor Gorge near Priddy

left to reach a gate at the entrance to the Ebbor Gorge Reserve. Continue downhill along the path through the woodland for 50 yards, before turning right to follow the path waymarked to 'The Gorge'. Follow this path down to a footbridge over a stream, then continue along the path as it bears right, all the while bordering the stream alongside in a gully. In 150 yards, turn left to continue following the path signposted to 'The Gorge' and follow what becomes an ever-steeper path climbing uphill between the limestone cliffs. In 1/4 mile, the steepest climb now behind you, turn right at a junction – the path is waymarked to the car park – and continue uphill for 40 yards to a crossroads.

## Fun Things to See and Do ◆

**Bears and wolves onced roamed Ebbor Gorge** and though these animals have long since gone, it should be possible to discover at least one or two badgers' setts alongside the footpaths. Certainly, the footprints left behind when they forage for food are clearly visible. From the viewpoint high above the gorge, buzzards may be spotted circling over the treetops whilst kestrels can often be seen hovering over the Mendip uplands. You might catch a glimpse of a sparrowhawk in search of food, speeding through the woodland. In springtime, the woodland floor is awash with traditional English wildflowers, which in turn attract any number of butterflies, including the white letter hairstreak.

Natural history, however, will take second place to the cliffs and rocks of the gorge itself. In one or two places, cracks have been widened to form very small caves, which at one time provided shelter for Stone Age people. These are fascinating places and archaeologists have unearthed many ancient tools and ornaments from these times, so young treasure seekers should keep their eyes peeled; you never know what you might find!

# Kiddiwalks near Bristol & Bath

❷ Turn right – still signed to the car park – and follow the path ahead for 100 yards to a junction, where the main path goes off on the left. Detour ahead at this point, however, for 50 yards to a spectacular clifftop viewpoint. Return the 50 yards to that junction, turn right and descend the hillside for 350 yards to a junction in the valley bottom.

Turn right and follow the footpath through the valley bottom, over a footbridge and up to the junction passed near the beginning of the walk. Turn right and follow the woodland path for 350 yards, keeping on the path as it eventually climbs steeply uphill to a stile and the top end of the car park by the information centre.

## ◆ Background Notes ◆

**Ebbor Gorge** is a National Nature Reserve, managed by the Nature Conservancy Council and leased from the National Trust. The gorge is typical of limestone country – it was carved out by an ancient river that has long since disappeared beneath the permeable limestone. Within the gorge, joints and fissures have been enlarged by the passage of rainwater, leaving behind small caves and rock shelters where the remains of reindeer, bears, wolves and lemmings have been found by archaeologists. Neolithic man also sought shelter in these caves around 3000 BC, and his various remains – bones, tools and ornaments – can be seen in Wells Museum.

The gorge is surrounded by deciduous woodland, which is both carefully managed and conserved by the Nature Conservancy Council. The woodland at the foot of the gorge contains ash, elm, beech and oak, together with herbaceous plants such as dog's mercury, enchanter's nightshade and hart's tongue fern. Badgers are plentiful here, and you may notice their tracks left when in search of berries and beetles. On the rather more rocky slopes of the gorge itself, vegetation characteristic of such an upland environment is found – dogwood, spindle, whitebeam and buckthorn. The excellent display centre next to the car park gives a full account of the natural history and geology of the area.

The view from the top of the cliffs above the gorge is truly spectacular. Here the path is some 800 feet above sea level, and spread out panoramically beneath are the Somerset Levels, Wookey and Wells, as well as the Tor at Glastonbury. In the distance, far away to the south and west, lie the Quantock Hills and Exmoor.

# 5

# Westhay Moor

## On the Level

The wetlands of Westhay Moor

In most parts of Britain, moors tend to be open upland – an exposed and forbidding landscape best suited to the hill-walker, to the Wainwrights of this world, rather than young children! Inhospitable territory such as Dartmoor immediately springs to mind. In Somerset, however, the moors are the areas of lowland that, prior to the advent of drainage schemes and flood defences, would have been marshland often prone to flooding when high tides swept up through the Bristol Channel. Deep in the heart of these moors – better known as the Somerset Levels – former peat workings near Westhay have been flooded to produce a wetland of world renown. The absence of any contours makes this perfect walking country and an ideal place to introduce youngsters to the delights of birdwatching.

# Kiddiwalks near Bristol & Bath

 **Getting there** *Follow the B3151 road from Glastonbury to Westhay, before continuing through the village towards Wedmore. In 1/2 mile, on a left-hand bend by a property called Turnpike House, turn right along a minor road signposted to Godney. In 1 1/4 miles, on a sharp right-hand bend, keep ahead along Dagg's Lane Drove and the Westhay Reserve parking area is on the right.*

**Length of walk** 3 miles
**Time** Allow about 2 hours for the walk.

**Terrain** Most young children would find this within their capabilities as the walk is completely level. It is also suitable for buggies, although the tracks and byways are slightly bumpy underfoot.
**Start/Parking** Westhay Reserve car park (GR 456437).
**Maps** OS Landranger 182 or OS Explorer 141.
**Refreshments** There are no refreshment facilities on this walk. Nearby Glastonbury, however, can boast cafés, teashops and restaurants aplenty and it is a fascinating town to visit. There is also a fine teashop at the nearby Peat Moors Visitor Centre – see below.

## ◆ Fun Things to See and Do ◆

 **Westhay Moor has several hides** from which children can be encouraged to do a spot of birdwatching. They will enjoy opening the flaps from within the hide, and peering out across the marshland and pools to spot the herons, mallards, swans, coots, and moorhens. At the end of your visit to Westhay, it is worth going to the **Peat Moors Visitors Centre** – signposted from Westhay – which has displays relating to the human and natural history of the local moors.

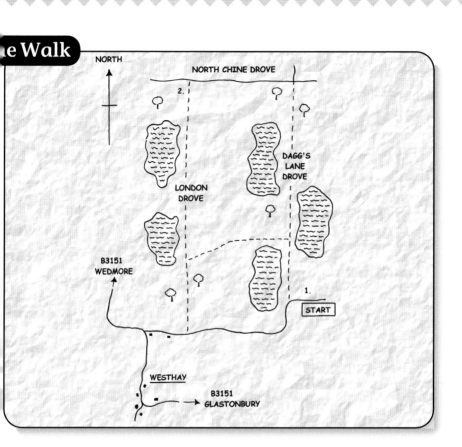

**1** Walk in a northerly direction along Dagg's Lane Drove for 350 yards, before passing through a kissing gate on the left bearing a sign that reads 'Foot access to London Drove and Hides'. Follow the main grassy path ahead between the flooded peat workings for 600 yards to a handgate and London Drove, making one or two detours to visit the hides.

Turn right, and follow London Drove northwards for 1 mile through areas of flooded peat workings and on across the moors to its junction with a quiet lane. This lane is shown on the 'Explorer' sheet as North Chine Drove.

**2** Turn right, and follow this lane for 500 yards to a minor crossroads. Turn right at this crossroads, and follow a track – Dagg's Lane Drove again – across the moors and between flooded peat workings for just over 1 mile back to the car park. A number of hides situated along the way make enjoyable detours.

## ♦ Background Notes ♦

**Westhay Moor was described** in the Middle Ages as being 'wet and weely, miry and moorish'. This is rather a gloomy picture for a landscape that has more recently been described as 'wild country ... fascinating and quite magical'. The second description is far closer to the truth! The damp, low-lying peat moor is criss-crossed by a network of drainage ditches, known locally as 'rhynes'. This watery environment provides a natural home for such diverse birdlife as swans, herons and kingfishers, whilst flocks of peewits are a common sight in the surrounding fields. Part of the exhausted peat working has been purchased by the Somerset Trust for Nature Conservation and is being developed as Greater Westhay Reserve. Alder and willow have been planted, and extensive reed beds developed. The Reserve has attracted badgers and foxes, kestrels and coots, as well as large numbers of dragonfly.

**Peat** – vegetable matter decomposed by water and partly carbonised by chemical change – has been worked for many years on the Somerset Levels. Traditionally hand-dug, the peat blocks were used in local homesteads as fuel. Today, peat extraction is a major business, with the product having a variety of horticultural uses. Controversy surrounds the industry, however, with the water table on the moors having to be lowered by pumping to facilitate peat extraction. This destroys the unique habitats in the area, with the conditions favoured by moisture-loving plants being gradually debased. Conservationists fear that, at current rates of extraction, the area could become little more than a collection of flooded pits in the ground in the not too distant future. The workings, however, are a fascinating sight, with the neatly stacked lines of peat blocks lying alongside extensive trenches filled with ebony-coloured water.

# 16

# Crook Peak

## On Top of the World

Atop Crook Peak

There is only one genuine 'peak' marked on the Ordnance Survey maps of the Bath and Bristol region ... and that is Crook Peak. Although rising to just 628 feet above sea level, this Mendip summit does have a genuine mountain feel to it. This is due in no small measure to the magnificent limestone outcrop that bedecks its summit. The views from this lofty hilltop perch are as spectacular as you would expect, ranging from the Bristol Channel and the distant Welsh Hills to the Quantock Hills, the Somerset Levels and Glastonbury Tor. It is a perfect spot to rest and linger awhile.

# Kiddiwalks near Bristol & Bath

*16*

**Getting there** *Follow the A38 south from Bristol for 15 miles before turning right into Cross. Having passed the New Inn, continue along this unclassified road for 1³/₄ miles until, just past Compton Bishop, the Crook Peak parking area is on the left-hand side of the road.*

**Length of walk** 2 miles
**Time** Allow about 2 hours for the walk.

**Terrain** This walk is better suited to slightly older children, rather than toddlers, with some climbs as well as the rock scramble at the summit.
**Start/Parking** The Crook Peak parking area (GR 393551).
**Maps** OS Landranger 182 or OS Explorer 153.
**Refreshments** With no refreshment facilities, take a picnic to enjoy on the limestone grassland around Crook Peak.

## ◆ Fun Things to See and Do ◆

**Crook Peak is one of the** finest viewpoints in the Bath and Bristol area. Stand on the rocky outcrop at the summit and look south, across the Somerset Levels. Reading from left to right you should be able to pick out Wavering Down, Cheddar Reservoir, Glastonbury Tor, Brent Knoll and the M5 motorway, Hinkley Point and Bridgwater Bay, the Bristol Channel and Brean Down. Further afield, the distant Welsh Hills are clearly visible on a fine day, as are the Quantock Hills in West Somerset. If geography lessons soon lose their appeal, the miniature limestone outcrops on Crook Peak are perfect for that first taste of rock climbing. Whilst it is always best for adults to be close at hand during these rock climbing exploits, the rocks are solid and stable, with no loose boulders with which to contend. The hilltop is also a quite perfect location for a picnic, an ideal 'carrot' to keep flagging spirits going on the climb to this Mendip vantage point.

◆◆◆◆◆◆◆◆◆◆◆◆◆◆◆◆◆◆◆◆◆◆◆◆◆◆◆◆◆◆◆◆◆◆◆◆◆

## e Walk

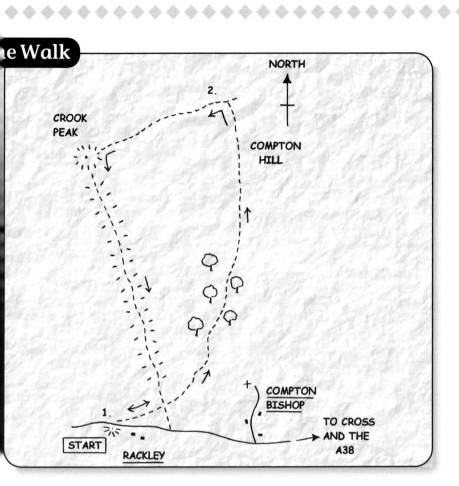

❶ From the car park, cross the road to a Crook Peak information board. Ignore the handgate beyond this board giving access to the open hillside – instead turn right to another handgate and join an enclosed track. Follow this track for 350 yards until it climbs to join an open grassy ridge coming down from Crook Peak.

Cross this ridge, and follow the track opposite that bears left into some woodland before dropping downhill to a junction of paths. At the fork ahead, keep to the lower right-hand path signposted to Compton Bishop, and continue for 40 yards to a gate. Just before this gate, bear left up to a wooden barrier and continue along the

# Kiddiwalks near Bristol & Bath

footpath that follows the bottom edge of the National Trust's Crook Peak property. All the while, there are views to the right across Compton Bishop towards Wavering Down. Continue along the footpath, climbing steadily uphill, to reach a dip in the hills some 1/2 mile distant.

❷ On reaching a hilltop wall and a broad grassy track running from east to west across the hilltop, turn left and continue the 250 yards to the rocky summit of Crook Peak, climbing a few rocks to secure the actual peak. Follow the grassy ridge running south-east from the summit for 3/4 mile, passing above Compton Bishop, to reach a wooden barrier. Beyond this barrier, turn right and retrace your steps along the track followed at the outset for 350 yards back to the handgate, information board and parking area.

## Background Notes ◆

**The hilltops above Compton Bishop** – which include **Crook Peak** and **Wavering Down** – were acquired by the National Trust in March 1986. The whole area is a 'Site of Special Scientific Interest' on account of its rich variety of grassland and woodland habitats, 719 acres of what is effectively commonland that lies within the Mendip Hills 'Area of Outstanding Natural Beauty'. Such designations are testimony indeed to the quality of the natural environment hereabouts, which has been described as 'a walker's delight with its short turf, wide views and wildlife'. This is undoubtedly some of the best scenery to be found on Mendip.

To travellers on the nearby M5 motorway, Crook Peak would appear to be the highest point on the Mendip Hills. In actuality, it falls 400 feet below the triangulation pillar on Blackdown, high above Burrington Combe, which at 1,067 feet above sea level is the true high point on Mendip. The name 'Crook' is due to the rocky outcrop at the summit, which is said to resemble a 'crook' or packhorse saddle. Such high landmarks inevitably became sites for beacons in centuries past. Confirmation of this fact can be found in the nearby village of Banwell, where the churchwarden's accounts for 1580 make interesting reading. A reference to the sum of 5 shillings 'pd the firste day of July for one load of wood for the Beaken and for carryinge of the same to Croke Peke' can be found. Some old Admiralty charts actually mark the Peak as 'see me not', an indication of its unreliability as a landmark. This can be put down to the fact that low cloud often envelops the summit.

# 17

# *Blackdown and Beacon Batch*

## *Summit Else!*

The ancient Forest of Mendip stretched from the North Somerset coast near Weston-super-Mare eastwards to Cottle's Oak on the fringes of Frome. It is West Mendip, however, that most attracts the interest of the guidebook writers. Here we find the best-known attractions – Cheddar Gorge and Burrington Combe, Wookey Hole and Ebbor Gorge. West Mendip is also the location of Beacon Batch, at 1,065 feet above sea level the literal high point on all Mendip. As well as the thrill of ascending one of the best-known summits in the West Country – relatively painlessly it must be said! – the open hillsides around this lofty hilltop perch are covered in bilberry plants in midsummer.

# Blackdown and Beacon Batch

◆ ◆ ◆ ◆ ◆ ◆ ◆ ◆ ◆ ◆ ◆ ◆ ◆ ◆ ◆ ◆ ◆ ◆ ◆ ◆ ◆ ◆ ◆ ◆ ◆

**Getting there** *From the A368 Weston to Booth road, follow the B3134 up through Burrington Combe from the Rock of Ages and the Burrington Inn. In 1 mile, at the head of Burrington Combe, there is a parking area on the left-hand side, 100 yards below Ellick House.*

**Length of walk** 2 miles
**Time** Probably no more than 1½ hours.
**Terrain** With most of the walk following hillside paths and tracks, this walk is not suitable for buggies and pushchairs. It is

a short – and relatively easy – climb onto one of the high points in Somerset, and could be tackled by the youngest of school-age children ... although the occasional piggyback will probably be needed!
**Start/Parking** The parking area at the head of Burrington Combe (GR 489581).
**Maps** OS Landranger 182 or OS Explorer 141.
**Refreshments** There are no refreshment facilities on the walk itself, but the Burrington Inn back down the B3134 in Burrington Combe is definitely family-friendly.

## e Walk

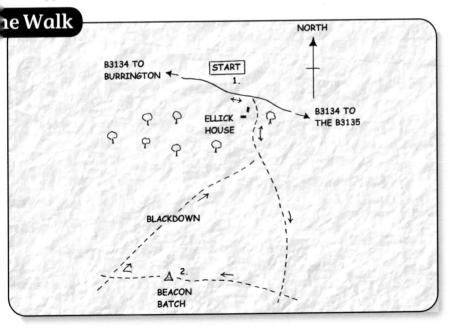

# Kiddiwalks near Bristol & Bath

◆ ◆ ◆ *17* ◆ ◆ ◆ ◆ ◆ ◆ ◆ ◆ ◆ ◆ ◆ ◆ ◆ ◆ ◆ ◆ ◆ ◆ ◆ ◆ ◆ ◆ ◆

❶ Cross to the verge opposite, turn left and follow the B3134 for 100 yards to Ellick House. Immediately past this property, turn right along a stony track and continue for 150 yards to the edge of the open hillside known as Blackdown. Turn left and follow the path running along the bottom left-hand edge of the hillside, a hedge on the left, for ½ mile to a gate and track on the

## ◆ Fun Things to See and Do ◆

**Blackdown is home to large** numbers of low-growing woody plants such as heather and gorse. The most appealing plant, however, is the whortleberry, better known in this country as the bilberry. The small black berries are much loved by the Americans, and are used in pies and with waffles. The berries are ripe enough to pick in July, which makes this an ideal time to visit this part of the Mendip Hills, just as long as you remember to pack a plastic container for the berries.

As you head across the ridge from the trig point on Blackdown, rows of small grassy mounds lying either side of the sandy path can be spotted. Many theories have been put forward to explain these series of bumps, ranging from them being synchronised molehills through to burial mounds! The most plausible suggestion is that these mounds are grassed-over boulders designed to destroy enemy planes tempted to land on this flat upland during the 1939-45 war.

On the drier and sunnier areas of the hillside, the occasional adder might be spotted. Blackdown, an area of dry heathland, is the perfect habitat for this poisonous snake as it lies in wait for the small mammals on which it preys. Do not be too worried by the prospect of poisonous snakes, however, and reassure the younger members of the party by pointing out that the adder is quite a timid creature that will quickly retreat if disturbed.

# Blackdown and Beacon Batch

left-hand side. At this point, turn right and follow a well-defined path uphill through the bracken and gorse for 600 yards to the trig point on Beacon Batch.

❷ Continue directly ahead along the narrow sandy path that runs the length of Blackdown's ridge. In 300 yards, where a bridlepath crosses the footpath at an angle, take a sharp right turn. Follow what is a grassy ride across the hilltop and on downhill to a marker post on the bottom edge of the open hillside. Beyond this post, retrace your steps along the stony track followed at the outset back to Ellick House and the B3134. Turn left to return to the parking area.

## Background Notes ◆

**Blackdown:** Whilst the predominant bedrock on Mendip is carboniferous limestone, on the very highest hilltops this has been eroded to expose the underlying old red sandstone. This change in geology – which occurs just above Ellick House where the walk joins the open hillsides of Blackdown – is marked by a clear change in vegetation types. The more acidic soils of the upland area support bracken and fern, gorse and heather, with the more traditional oak and ash, blackthorn and bramble being found lower down the valley in Burrington Combe itself.

**Beacon Batch** The 1,000-foot contour is only reached at two other locations on these hills – Pen Hill above Wells and North Hill above Priddy. From the trig point on Beacon Batch, the views are – as one would expect – quite exceptional. To the north, beyond the Chew Valley and its reservoirs, lie Bristol International Airport and the fringes of the city itself, whilst to the south one can see the Quantock Hills and the distant whalebacks of Exmoor. Most eyes, however, will be drawn in a westerly direction towards the coast. Close at hand are Weston-super-Mare, Brean Down and Brent Knoll, whilst beyond the Bristol Channel lie the outlines of the Brecon Beacons and the Black Mountains. It is quite simply a fine spot to rest and linger awhile.

# 18

# Cleeve and Goblin Combe

## Lightness and Darkness

A dark and shady combe, with dense woodland that lies beneath rock faces and scree slopes, gives an almost eerie start to this walk in North Somerset. It is not too long, however, before the veil of gloom is lifted and the footpaths climb onto the clifftops high above this secluded valley. The sunny and airy limestone grassland – with extensive views across the surrounding landscape – produces an almost uplifting feel. Goblin Combe is a peaceful out-of-the-way nature reserve, owned and managed by the Avon Wildlife Trust, with a particular reputation for its rich variety of butterflies.

# Cleeve and Goblin Combe

Getting there *Follow the A370 south from Bristol for 10 miles to Cleeve, before taking a left turn into Cleeve Hill Road, just before the Lord Nelson pub. The car park lies 200 yards along this road on the left, alongside an old quarry.*

**Length of walk** 2½ miles
**Time** Allow up to 2 hours
**Terrain** The walk through the combe itself would be suitable for modern 'all-terrain' buggies, although the climb onto the clifftops can only be tackled on foot. It is probably best to hold hands with younger children on the section across the clifftops above Goblin Combe.

## Fun Things to See and Do ◆

**Goblin Combe is an excellent place** for a visit if you want to nurture an interest in nature and wildlife. In the dark woodland lie any number of fascinating plants, including the very rare moonwort fern, whilst on the clifftops high above the trees, many different wild flowers can be found growing – anything from bell heather to autumn lady's tresses. The flowers in turn attract butterflies, and over 30 different species have been recorded on the site. So, be sure to have a flower or butterfly book to hand in order to answer the constant query of 'What's that?'.

Goblin Combe lies on the flight path into Bristol International Airport. As you follow the clifftop path above the combe, low-flying planes will be seen quite literally just overhead! Many of the planes are operated by Easyjet, with incoming flights from holiday destinations in Southern Europe, whilst the smaller British Airways jets are flying on business routes to and from France, Holland and Germany. With a pair of binoculars you will enjoy some real close up views of these magnificent flying machines and perhaps the passengers will be delighted to see small hands waving at them from below.

# Kiddiwalks near Bristol & Bath

## 18

**Start/Parking** The parking area near the entrance to Goblin Combe (GR 459654).
**Maps** OS Landranger 172 or OS Explorer 154.
**Refreshments** Youngsters who

manage this walk can be rewarded at journey's end with a visit to the Lord Nelson in Cleeve, one of the 'Hungry Horse' chain of inns aimed at families.

## The Walk

❶ Leave the car park, then turn right for just 20 yards before turning right into Plunder Street, initially passing the Goblin Combe Centre. Almost immediately, keep left at a fork and follow a driveway along to the entrance to Walnut Tree Farm on the left. Pass through the gateway into the Goblin Combe Estate. Follow the main path ahead. In ³/₄ mile, pass a wall,

steps and information board on the left and continue through the combe. In another ¹/₄ mile, ignore the path going off on the right, keeping ahead instead for 300 yards to a clearing and junction of paths in an area of coniferous trees.

❷ Turn left along a side path for 150 yards, before following a faint path on the left that climbs uphill

# Cleeve and Goblin Combe

into the woodland. In 150 yards, keep on this path as it bears right, running parallel to an old boundary wall on the left, and continue up to a clearing and some farm buildings. Immediately before these buildings, turn left along a path running past an information board and continue for 100 yards to a stile and an open hilltop high above the combe. Follow the clifftop path ahead – it is rocky in places – for 400 yards, keeping on the path as it drops downhill to join a stepped path. Turn left and follow this path downhill into the valley bottom, descending some steep steps at the end. Join the main track through the combe, turn right and retrace your steps back to the parking area.

## Background Notes ◆

**Goblin Combe** is a delightful nature reserve whose origins can be traced back to a time when melting snow and ice were moulding the landscape. This is a reserve of great variety, with the sunny and airy grasslands above contrasting strongly with the dark, eerie combe below. The combe is wooded and damp, and is home to the rare and unusual moonwort fern, which can be found growing under the older yew trees. This succulent fern, usually less than 6 inches tall, takes its name from its moon-shaped leaflets. Its rarity can be gauged from the fact that **Botrychium lunaria** is said to be more commonly found in fable and lore than growing in the wild!

High above the combe lies an area of open limestone grassland and heath. The grassland is at its best in late summer, when flora such as autumn gentian, autumn lady's tresses and yellow-wort appear, whilst the heath reaches its colourful peak during high summer, when the bell heather is in bloom. The rich flora in turn attracts a vast collection of butterflies, with over 30 different species having been recorded. These include the grizzled and dingy skippers, brown argus and green hairstreak. In order to maintain the quality of the grassland and heath, and to prevent the spread of larger plants, the Avon Wildlife Trust is encouraging rabbits to encroach on the site, so that they will nibble down any larger plants that grow.

# 19

# *Sand Point and Middle Hope*

## *The Bristol Channel Coast*

N orth of Weston-super-Mare, the limestone promontory of Middle Hope and Sand Point projects finger-like into the Bristol Channel, and we find some real cliffs – albeit in miniature – falling away into the sea. This most beautiful stretch of coastline now comes under the watchful eye of the National Trust, thereby preserving it from the rash of commercial development that has engulfed nearby Sand Bay. This is without doubt the finest section of coastline within a short drive of Bath and Bristol, commanding magnificent views across the Bristol Channel towards the islands of Steep Holm and Flat Holm, and beyond to Wales and the Brecon Beacons.

# Sand Point and Middle Hope

**Getting there** *Leave the M5 at junction 21 and head towards Weston-super-Mare. In 400 yards, follow the B3440 signposted to Sand Bay. Initially, the signposted route passes through housing estates before following a country lane to the sea front at Sand Bay. Turn right on reaching the sea front and continue to the end of what is a cul-de-sac road to reach the car park.*

**Length of walk** 2½ miles

**Time** Allow 2 hours

**Terrain** With its cliffs and rocky outcrops, this walk is designed for older – more adventurous – youngsters. Toddlers would need to be well-controlled!

**Start/Parking** The National Trust car park for Sand Point and Middle Hope (GR 331660).

**Maps** OS Landranger 182 or OS Explorer 153.

**Refreshments** Grandma's Tea Room lies alongside the sea front road heading back to the motorway from Middle Hope and Sand Point.

## Fun Things to See and Do ◆

**Sand Point and Middle Hope** is a rocky headland protruding into the Bristol Channel. Amongst the landmarks that you should be able to point out are the islands of Steep Holm and Flat Holm, the Severn bridges and the Welsh coast. The headland is an excellent viewpoint for spotting sea birds, whilst the rocky beaches are ideal for searching for small maritime animals. Of more significance are the rocks themselves, this being one of only three places in England where volcanic rock can be found within a layer of limestone. 'Tuffs' – volcanic ash deposits – and lavas showing what are described as 'pillow structures' can be seen around the headland. I imagine that the main attraction, however, would be the small rocky bays where there are thousands of pebbles and stones for skimming across the water, trying to recreate the bouncing bomb effect. It is possible to go paddling, but be aware that just offshore is a layer of thick sticky mud!

# Kiddiwalks near Bristol & Bath

## The Walk

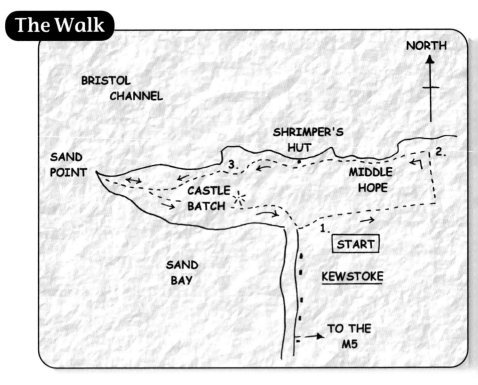

❶ Leave the car park and follow the unmetalled road, signposted 'footpath only – no through road', that bears sharply to the right. In 100 yards, follow a stepped path on the left waymarked 'to the headland' and climb to a gate on the hilltop. Turn right and follow a fence on the right for 550 yards to the corner of the field, before bearing left to follow the end field boundary down to a gate and stepped stile on the right, the Bristol Channel lying directly ahead.

❷ Turn left and follow a grassy path above a small pebbly bay, shortly dropping down a rocky scramble to the bay itself. Continue following a grassy path along the edge of the hilltop immediately above the sea for ¹/₂ mile to a point where the path ends and cliffs lie ahead. At this point, bear left to a gate and stile.

❸ Follow the path uphill above the cliffs, and onto the western tip of Sand Point. Retrace your steps back along the ridge to a fork.

# Sand Point and Middle Hope

Ignore the left fork – the path followed earlier – keeping directly ahead instead along the ridge. Having passed a rocky outcrop, continue to Castle Batch and the trig point. Follow the path that bears right beyond the trig point before sloping downhill to some steps and the road by the car park.

## Background Notes ◆

**Middle Hope and Sand Point,** a limestone peninsula north of Weston-super-Mare, is an area steeped in history. Across the flat hilltop there are traces of banks thought to represent early pre-historic field systems. Archaeological excavations have revealed two Iron Age settlements, Romano-British pottery fragments and a 4th-century coin of the Valentinian period. Castle Batch is a Norman motte, whose mound and ditch were unfortunately disturbed during wartime construction work at the site.

At one time, Sand Point and Middle Hope probably formed an island, only accessible at low tide across the surrounding mudflats. This would have made it a fine site for defensive settlement, and would therefore explain its long history of human habitation. Shrimping took place on the mudflats during the 19th and early 20th century, with the shrimper's hut being a relic from this period. The shrimps were brought to the hut and boiled in a copper pot, before being dried and sold in Weston. At low tide, the wooden fishing poles from which nets were hung can still be seen offshore.

Many years ago, lead-mining activity took place on Middle Hope, and several of the old tracks hereabouts represent the courses of old tramways. Mining shafts have been discovered over the years, and one such 'secret tunnel', uncovered by Boy Scouts in the 1930s, was immediately filled in for safety reasons. The area was also the scene of the 'Secret War' during the 1939-45 hostilities. Unusual experiments took place on Middle Hope that involved a pair of high-speed catapult tracks laid down for missile testing. The missiles were – at the time – said to be 'unlike any seen in the history of modern warfare'.

# 20

# *Clevedon and Wain's Hill*

*Oh I Do Like To Be Beside The Seaside!*

W hat could be better than a day at the coast, with the opportunity to paddle, play with pebbles, climb rocks and enjoy an ice cream or two! This walk is based around Clevedon, a traditional Victorian seaside resort overlooking the Bristol Channel. From the promenade, the route climbs onto Church Hill and Wain's Hill, an upland area that forms a headland to the south of the town, before following a tarmac path around the headland itself. Designated as 'The Poet's Walk' on account of its popularity with Coleridge when he resided in the town, the views across the Channel towards Wales and along the promenade to the local pier will inspire even the most unpoetic into verse! The prospect of a couple of hours playing on the beach at the end of the walk should spur young legs to take the route in their stride.

# Clevedon and Wain's Hill

**⊛ Getting there** *From junction 20 on the M5 motorway, follow the signs to Clevedon's sea front. Within 200 yards of a sharp right turn that sees the road heading parallel to the foreshore, separated from it by a large grassed play area, park on the roadside by the Little Harp Inn. This will prove a tempting refreshment stop at journey's end.*

**Length of walk** 2 miles
**Time** Allow about 1½ hours for the walk.
**Terrain** Most of the walk follows tarmac paths, so it is easy going for pushchairs, although the fold up design would be best as they will need to be carried across Church Hill.

**Start/Parking** Clevedon's sea front by the Little Harp Inn (GR 399714).

**Maps** OS Landranger 172 or OS Explorer 154.

**Refreshments** Being a seaside resort, Clevedon can boast teashops and cafés, pubs and restaurants aplenty. The Little Harp Inn at journey's end is the most convenient destination, however.

## Fun Things to See and Do ◆

**The beach at Clevedon** is the ideal place to hunt for sea creatures. Look out for a dog whelk, a carnivorous creature whose main prey is the barnacle. Barnacles are, of course, those small light-grey domed shells that often cover rocks so completely that there is hardly a space between them. Several thousand barnacles can crowd into a square yard of space – making them, not surprisingly, the most common animal on rocky shores. More exciting will be the discovery of a hermit crab. An apparently empty winkle or whelk shell inspected more closely may reveal a small crab's claw blocking the entrance. If the shell is placed on the beach and watched quietly, the occupant will eventually emerge and scuttle away from its borrowed home.

# Kiddiwalks near Bristol & Bath

## 20

### The Walk

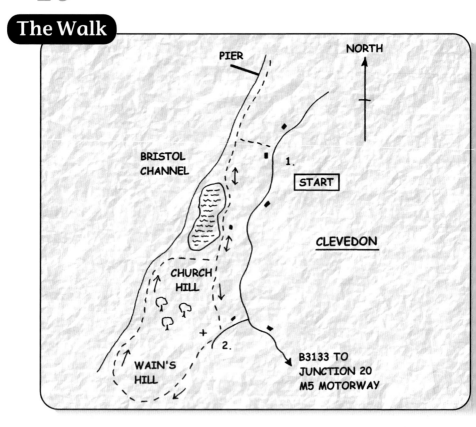

❶ Walk across to the promenade beyond the Little Harp and turn left. At the far end of the prom, climb the steps into the woodland to begin following 'The Poet's Walk'. Ignoring any side turnings, climb to the top of Church Hill, where the tree cover is left behind and open views begin to appear. Cross to the far side of the hilltop and follow a path on the left down to a tarmac path. Follow this path to the right along to St Andrew's church and continue down to Old Church Road.

❷ Turn right and, in 200 yards, pass through a gateway, with a small boatyard ahead. Almost immediately, turn right onto the path that climbs Wain's Hill. Follow this path to the south-western tip of the headland, where a seat commands views across the Channel. From the tip of the headland, continue following the path around the coast and back towards Clevedon. Keep on this path all of the way back to the old boating lake, where the path bears to the right to rejoin the promenade. It is now a simple matter of retracing your steps to the end of the walk.

## Background Notes ◆

**Clevedon** sits sedately overlooking the Bristol Channel, on a rocky and pebbly stretch of the coastline. The atmosphere is very Victorian, with large grey limestone villas, public parks and bowling greens, although Georgian and Regency buildings speak of the town's gradual development from a fishing village to a small, fashionable resort during the 19th century. The town has links with such literary figures as the novelist William Thackeray, and the poets Samuel Taylor Coleridge and Lord Tennyson. Tennyson's closest friend at Cambridge had been Arthur Hallam, nephew of Sir Charles Elton of Clevedon Court. Tennyson's well-known poem *In Memoriam* was written in the year that he visited Hallam's tomb in Clevedon. It is a poem full of classic quotations, including the immortal:

### *'Tis better to have loved and lost, Than to never have loved at all.*

**Clevedon Pier**, the town's most famous Victorian landmark, was constructed in 1869 of iron rails originally intended for use on Brunel's South Wales Railway. The pier, unfortunately, collapsed in October 1970 during a periodic safety check, leaving its pavilion standing forlornly at sea. Appeals were launched for its restoration and supported by a number of celebrities including Sir John Betjeman. Of Clevedon Pier he wrote: 'It recalls a painting by Turner, or an etching by Whistler or Sickert, or even a Japanese print ... Without its pier, Clevedon would be a diamond with a flaw.'

A Pier Trust was formed and, with major financial contributions from the Historic Buildings Council and the National Heritage Memorial Fund, structural work was completed in 1988. The historic Victorian pier is now fully open to the public and, following the many years of work invested in its restoration, no visitor should begrudge the entrance toll!

# Birds to see along the way

KINGFISHER

NIGHTINGALE

MALLARD

CURLEW

REDSHANK

COMMON
TERN

HERON

DUNLIN

CORMORANT